MAGNIFICENT MACRAMÉ

Marie-Jeanine Solvit

MAGNIFICENT MACRAMÉ

STERLING
PUBLISHING CO., INC. NEW YORK

Oak Tree Press Co., Ltd.
Distributed by WARD LOCK, Ltd., London & Sydney

Text and diagrams by Marie-Jeanine Solvit
Photographs by Philippe Jalladaud and Patrice Vérès

First published in the United States of America in 1979 by
Sterling Publishing Co., Inc., Two Park Avenue,
New York, N.Y. 10016
Published in Canada by Saunders of Toronto, Ltd.

Library of Congress Catalog Card no: 78-66295
ISBN 0—8069—5390—X Trade
        0—8069—5391—8 Library

IBM set in Great Britain by 𝗙\ Tek-Art
and printed in Italy

Contents

Introduction

Makrama is a Turkish word meaning 'scarf' or 'fringed napkin'.
Migramah is an Arab word meaning 'veil'.
Macramé is a Genoese term for 'knot'.

Macramé, the art of knotting, depends on 'see-through' effects and almost always includes fringes, thus retaining the meanings of its three root-words. It is a simple craft that uses one very basic material. It probably originated in the Near East, where as long ago as the ninth century BC warriors wore tunics edged with knotted fringes. People of all civilizations have loved ornament. All over the world macramé has been used to decorate clothes, for head-dresses, neck pieces, and so on, in ritual wear, and as furnishings and trimmings.

Sailors have often enlivened their isolation at sea by making things from cord and rope for barter at ports of call in India and China; maritime museums have some fine pieces of maritime macramé.

Suddenly, after almost disappearing, macramé returned towards the end of the last century and seems to have been thought of as a novelty.

Furnishings, trimmings and braids, rose-shaped mats, and collars for little girls were produced. They were worked either on padded cushions — the bottoms of which had screw clamps for attaching to a table edge — or on 'macramé supports', which were also screwed to the table to keep the 'holding cord' (the starting point of the work) in perfect horizontal tension.

The threads used for macramé during this period were very fine: yarn, thin braid or perlé cotton. The repetitive ease of the motifs, and the very high quality of the knotting, give these works an almost mechanical perfection.

Then macramé was forgotten once again. But it soon made a come-back when people realised that a vast range of new designs and applications was possible. The variety became greater, and macramé began to emerge as an art-form in its own right.

With the help of this book, you can now explore the full potential of macramé. It can be as abstract as any pure expressive form. You can combine lines, materials, space and colors in a non-figurative way. Compare the joining of different knots to the union of sounds in music. As the threads dance, intertwine, trap and then release one another, pursue each other and then come together again in your hands, you can produce objects of great decorative and practical value.

A clear diagram is better than a long explanation

Lark's head knot

Reverse lark's head knot

Double knot
(half hitch)

Overhand knot (bead
knot)

Vertical double knot
(half hitch)

Alternate double knot
(half hitch)

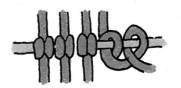

Horizontal double knot
bar (horizontal cording)

Diagonal double knot
bar (diagonal cording)

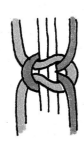

Flat knot (square knot)

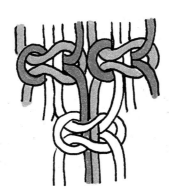

Alternating flat knots

Start of horizontal
double knot bar, using
the first thread as
leader

Single knotted chain

Central holding cord
with working threads
lying in opposite
directions

Japanese knot

Gathering knot
(collecting knot)

Joséphine knot

Experience required

You can see from a glance at the number of flat knot symbols which appear at the head of each chapter how easy or difficult it is to make the items described in this book.

One knot: suitable for beginners.

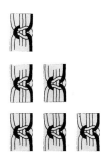

Two knots: for those already familiar with the technique.

Three knots: for those quite expert at macramé.

This indication of the ability required will save you from unpleasant surprises, but do not be discouraged by projects marked with three knots. The difficulty is either the length and number of threads to control or in the bulkiness of the item, for the basic knots remain the same. Perhaps the word should be simply 'patient', not 'expert', since all you need do is follow the instructions.

There is a glossary at the back of the book. Perhaps you should read through this glossary before you begin any projects, to familiarize yourself with the macramé terms used throughout this book. Also be sure to refer to the glossary while you are working, for explanations and directions for some of the terms used to make these projects.

Basic equipment

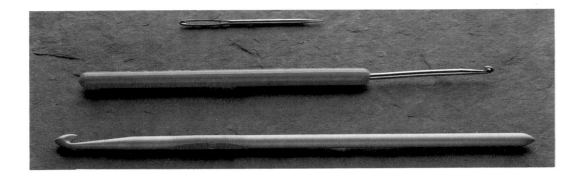

A board made of soft wood or thick insulation board (if the only material you have is too hard, you can glue one or more pieces of cork on top) into which you can stick the pins used to hold parts of the work temporarily in position. This is the knotting board.

Large-headed pins such as dressmaker's pins with colored glass heads, or special macramé T-pins or possibly even very fine nails.

A large sheet of graph paper to attach to the knotting board to help keep your lines perfectly horizontal or vertical when working on small and medium-sized pieces of macramé.

Scissors

Tape measure

Threads, which must always be strong and must not stretch.

The threads most frequently used are: macramé string, netting string, cord, sisal, jute, cotton, rug wool,(yarn), parcel twine coton perlé (pearl cotton).

Many other strings, wools and cottons may be added to this list, not forgetting leather thonging which is useful for certain projects. Beginners are strongly advised not to use stretchy or loosely twisted thread for macramé.

Other accessories

Embroidery needles and a crochet hook for darning in threads when finishing off certain items.

Dowelling rod, sticks, lengths of wood in round or square section, which will be used sometimes as thread bearers when starting off a piece of work, sometimes as horizontal rods when the work is under way.

Graduated rule to check spacing or ensure you are keeping different sections of the work the same distance apart.

Beads which are used to trim some of the items.

Rings for using as thread bearers or, bound with thread, as circular motifs in the body of the work.

Transparent glue to give added strength when finishing some of the items.

Many other accessories will also be used in the make-up of different macramé designs, but they fulfil the needs of specific projects and do not come under the heading of general accessories.
Indeed, we shall see that in order to reproduce certain designs in this book, we shall have to find accessories such as lampshade frames, wooden frames and other skeleton shapes. But these are special items which do not form a part of the accepted macramé equipment. I would add an accessory which is an idea of my own. It is easy enough to find and very useful in certain projects: a pair of table tennis net supports. You can screw these down very securely at the required distance apart; they allow you to start off a macramé project of considerable size (a blind for a picture window, for instance) on a long, perfectly-taut holding cord.
Finally, a little trick makes it easier to use threads which often tangle and which are numbered according to the order in which they were mounted on the holding cord: put a numbered wooden clothes peg (pin) on the end of each thread. Then you can pick out the threads very quickly.

Nautical bracelet

This is the simplest item of all to make.
It is the result of my son's first attempt at macramé.
Make it up quickly and you have an attractive bracelet
to give as a gift.

Design: Marie-Jeanine SOLVIT

The nylon cord used to make this bracelet and the shackle, which acts as a clasp, are sold at ships' supply shops. There is no need to worry about the bracelet getting wet, so you do not have to leave the key to your boat or locker behind when you enter the water - just hang it on the bracelet.

Materials

2m (2¼ yd) nylon cord and a shackle.

Method

Measure the circumference of the chosen wrist, allowing for the bracelet to fit loosely. Fold the cord in two. Pass the two loose ends over the rounded part of the shackle and pull them through until the distance between the looped end and the edge of the shackle equals the circumference of the wrist.
First make a flat knot, using as core threads the two which come from the looped end, and as knotting threads the two loose ends you put through the shackle. Pull very tight and continue with the flat knots until all that is left of the core is a round loop at the end of the work. Hook this on to the shackle.
To finish off, burn the end of the threads with a cigarette lighter. The nylon will shrivel and adhere to the last flat knot. You now have a very strong bracelet.

Christmas tree decorations

Children wait impatiently for Christmas. Some of them hang an
Advent calendar on their bedroom wall; this is a picture with 24
little paper windows to open, one for each day between 1 and 25
December, revealing a new picture each time and thus helping
children to count the days before Christmas.

You can make something along the same lines: on a large sheet of
drawing paper (or something similar) draw 24 numbered squares,
each at least 15 cm (6 in.) high by 10 cm (4 in.) wide.

Each day, starting on December 1, one of your children makes a
macramé Christmas tree decoration. If you have several children,
they can take it in turns. If they are too young, let them watch you
doing it; then they can learn their numbers by hanging each
decoration in its numbered box.

Materials

Odds and ends of knitting wool or yarn in bright colors; pipe
cleaners which, though flexible, are rigid enough to hold a shape;
long matchsticks; wooden beads; and, if possible, gold lamé knitting
yarn and some rings.

Join two pipe cleaners together end to end to make them long enough
and use them as the core for the shapes. Beads will hang from the
center on either gold threads or the same yarn as the surround.

Method

Use simple flat knots, tied tightly against each other to hide the
pipe cleaner core. Bend back one end of the pipe cleaner so that you
can hang it on a branch of the Christmas tree. This is how to make
the bright blue circle and the red triangle.

Design: Marie-Jeanine SOLVIT

The other red decoration is mounted on a long matchstick, along which you lay a double length of red thread and pass it through a bead at either end of the matchstick. Make two ends into a single knotted chain above the match and join them with an overhand knot so that you can hang the decoration. Mount 8 pieces of red wool 1.20 m (4 ft) long and make braids of flat knots, longer ones in the middle, finishing each one with a bead held in place by an overhand knot.

The orange decoration is started in the same way as the preceding one. As the wool is thicker, I have passed only a single length

through each bead at the ends of the match-stick, and the loop for hanging the decoration is trimmed with overhand knots 1 cm (¼ in.) apart. Use 4 pieces 1.40 m (4½ ft) long to make two braids of 7 flat knots joined together at the bottom in trellis pattern interlacing (see the glossary— and finished off with overhand knots. Wind wool tightly round the middle of the matchstick to cover it completely.

To finish this shield-shaped decoration, loop a length of wool over the middle of the matchstick and pass both ends through one bead. Thread a further bead onto each end, and finish with an overhand knot 2 cm below the first bead.

The lemon-coloured decoration is mounted in the same way as the last two, this time on a cross made with two matchsticks tied together with yellow wool at the middle. Leave the threads to hang it by unknotted and join the four ends joined over the middle with an overhand knot. The oval beads used here are of olive wood.

Mount 6 pieces 1 m long on each arm of the cross and make 3 braids of flat knots between 4 and 6.5 cm (1½-2½ in.) long, the longer ones in the middle. Finish by threading a wooden bead through the core threads of each braid of flat knots and holding it place with an overhand knot.

Design: Marie-Jeanine SOLVIT

The white **decoration** has a 3 cm (1¼ in.) diameter ring as thread bearer on which are mounted 24 pieces 80 cm (32 in.) long. Make 8 flat knots for each braid, ending with a bead held in place with an overhand knot. Stretch a thread across the middle of the ring. Mount on it two threads more than twice the length of the braids surrounding them so that the beads knotted on the four ends hang below in the center. Tie the ends of the first thread for a hanging loop.

The decoration in lamé knitting yarn is mounted on a matchstick like the preceding ones. A single knotted chain embellishes the hanging cord.
Join the 'windmill' motifs (see the glossary) together at the base with curved diagonal cording (double knot bars). The ends of the thread make a fringe, with 4 overhand knots on each.
Now you try to create some other decorations using this very simple technique right up to the 25th, when the Christmas tree will have some new **decorations**.

Small mural

*This project is a simple starter
before you launch
into more complex models.
It will look especially decorative in a
narrow space, on
a supporting pillar or in a recess hiding a run of pipes.
It also looks delightful in a child's room.*

Materials

105 m (115 yd) ordinary light-colored parcel string, 8 blond oblong wooden beads, 15 blond round wooden beads, a 40 cm (16 in.) length of thin bamboo.

Method

Mount 12 threads 8.50 m (28 ft) long on the bamboo bearer in double reverse lark's head (i.e. work in reverse lark's head, then with the same threads make a single half hitch each side of each knot.) With a piece of the same string introduced as leader work 2 rows of horizontal, double knot bars the leader making a half turn at the right-hand side. Next use threads 7 and 8, 19 and 20 as leaders for making up two diamonds in double diagonal cording (bars).

Trellis

Below the diamonds work a horizontal double knot bar on an inserted leader thread. Working from left to right, make a motif of staggered braids of 4 flat knots with the first 8 threads. Two oblong beads, each threaded onto 2 threads, frame the middle braid. With the next 4 threads work 9 diagonal cording double knot bars in groups of three, left to right, right to left, left to right. Reproduce these two motifs symmetrically on the right. Work 2 more horizontal double knot bars with an inserted leader thread. Now make 6 flat knots. Thread a round bead onto each pair of knotting threads, leaving threads 1 and 24 hanging free. Make a second row of 6 flat knots. Repeat the bead row and the flat knot row once more. Follow this with 2 horizontal double knot bars with an

inserted leader. Use thread 1 as leader for a diagonal double knot bar working across 7 threads from left to right, right to left, left to right. Using thread 9 as leader, work 3 rows of spaced diagonal double knot bars over 3 threads from left to right and then 3 rows from right to left. Reproduce these 2 motifs symmetrically on the right.

Work 1 complete horizontal knot bar on an inserted leader. Now work 'stepped' horizontal double knot bars on the 8 left-hand threads as follows:

1) Use thread 1 as leader for knotting threads 2, 3 and 4, starting from left to right.

2) Use thread 8 as leader for knotting threads 7, 6 and 5, starting from right to left.

After 6 rows of the "stepped" horizontal double knot bars, repeat the work in the opposite direction (from right to left and from left to right) to form 6 more bars. These 2 braids cross each other before meeting up again on the complete horizontal double knot bar at their base.

In the middle of this section, threads 9 and 10 pass through an oblong bead, as do threads 15 and 16. Work the 4 middle threads into 4 flat knots and a half flat knot and tie 2 alternating flat knots on the threads coming out of the beads. Work the 2nd half of this section in the same way, starting off with a half flat knot.

Reproduce the "stepped" horizontal double knot bars on threads 17-24. Work 2 horizontal double knot bars below this section on an inserted leader. Follow this with 6 spiral braids of 6 half flat knots (the half flat knots automatically spiral as you make them).

Then work 2 final horizontal double knot bars, again on an inserted leader.

Now make 6 flat knots. Leaving the core threads and also threads 1 and 24 free, thread a round bead onto each pair of knotting threads. Make 2 flat knots below each of the 6 above. Then, taking the threads in pairs, work on each a single knotted chain of 8 knots, securing them at the bottom with transparent glue.

Design: Maryse DUBOULOIS

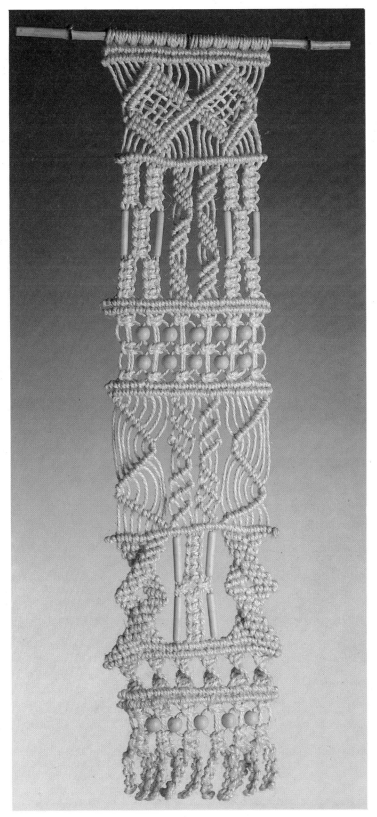

Wall umbrella-holder

*This simple project was made by
a 16 year old boy.*

Design: Marie-Jeanine SOLVIT

This unusual item will liven up a wall in an entrance hall, whether it stays empty or is filled with umbrellas. It has the added advantage that its owners have to put away their umbrellas dry — the only sure way of keeping them in tip-top condition for any length of time. You can also use the curved handle of your umbrella as a hat stand if you twist it into the right position.

Materials

1 piece of cane about 50 cm long (20 in.) to use as thread bearer.
24 large beads (those shown here are caramel colored ceramic)
72 m (80 yd) of thick brown sports wool
154 m (170 yd) of the same wool in a natural color

Method

Mount the threads on the cane bearer in the following order using reverse lark's head:
2 brown threads 2.40 m (3 yd) long

1 brown thread 9 m (10 yd) long
2 brown threads 2.40 m (3 yd) long
Using double reverse lark's head knots
(see page 20):
4 natural threads 9.60 m (10½ yd) long
2 brown threads 11 m (12 yd) long
8 natural threads 9.60 m (10½ yd) long
2 brown threads 11 m (12 yd) long
4 natural threads 9.60 m (10½ yd) long
Finish with 5 brown threads symmetrical with the 1st 5. Leave the brown threads hanging at either end for now.
Work 3 rows of alternating flat knots. The knotting threads of the last brown flat knots (those nearest to the middle) will be the leaders for diagonal double knot bars running down to meet in the middle. At this point, the brown threads reappear, covered with a natural colored half flat knot, and frame a bead with 2 overhand knots. Then, after being used as core threads of a natural flat knot, the brown threads separate into leaders for rows of double knot bars symmetrical with those above.
The brown thread sections each hold 3 beads.

Slide them onto the middle thread of each group of three, separating them with 3 vertical half hitches worked alternately with the lateral threads.

Work a flat knot under the last half hitch with the returning 4th brown thread.

Now work with the natural threads. With them, make braids of 4 alternating flat knots, then 1 central flat knot and 2 alternating flat knots, which brings the work level with the brown flat knot.

Using the natural threads from the diagonal double knot bars in the middle of the work, make 2 knots of a simple knotted chain, then 3, 4 and 5; and 5, 4, 3 and 2.

Now continue with the alternating flat knots again, adding the rings through which the umbrellas will be slipped as follows:

5 rows of alternating flat knots
2 brown rings of 11 flat knots (make these rings using the bead knot technique described in the *Glossary*)
8 rows of alternating flat knots
2 brown rings
6 rows of alternating flat knots
2 brown rings
8 rows of alternating flat knots
2 brown rings
7 rows of alternating flat knots

Work 2 rows of diagonal double knot bars running down to the middle, using the same threads as for the diagonals above. Tie a natural flat knot over the brown core threads, followed by a brown overhand knot, a bead and a brown overhand knot. Frame 2 more beads one after the other in this way using those same threads.

Add more beads, holding them in place with overhand knots on the threads, which should be divided up as follows (from the middle working out to either side):

3 threads, 2 threads, 2 threads, 2 brown threads, 3 threads, 2 threads, 3 threads.

The brown thread left over should be finished off at the back of the work using a fine crochet hook.

All that remains to do is to make the brown borders. The 2 long threads in the middle should be knotted around the lateral threads in vertical half hitches, crossing over each other regularly in the middle between each half hitch. The half hitch nearest the middle of the work should catch up a natural thread here and there to tie the border to the natural middle section. To finish, do this level with each of the brown rings so that it will be hidden behind an umbrella. Tie the threads of each brown border into a large overhand knot at the bottom of the panel and cut them at an angle in line with the beaded border.

Curtain tie-back

*This quick, easy piece of work gives a
decorative finish to your curtains
even if you have several windows to cover.*

Materials

Hemp
1 holding cord 0.95 m (1 yd) long
44 threads 1.50 m (1½ yd) long
7 fairly large ceramic beads chosen to match
the color of your room

Method

Mount the 44 threads on the holding cord in
double reverse lark's head knots (see page 20).
Work 2 rows of alternating flat knots. Now
work 3 V shapes of flat knots so that each
side of the V has 5 slanting flat knots. The
bottom of these V's should lie below the 7th,
the 12th, the 17th flat knots of the 1st row.
Slanting flat knots form half a V-shape at
either end of the work.

1st motif: Take as leader the core threads
of each of the highest flat knots (they are in
the 2nd row) and delineate the V of flat
knots with diagonal double knot bars.
Next take up the 2 highest threads in the
broken line of delineation. They become
leaders of bars of diagonal double knots
parallel with the broken line.
Work with 4 threads on each row of knots.
Continue these rows of parallel bars using as
leaders the threads which are at the middle

of the motif. The 1st row has 4 knotting
threads and the last row 1 knotting thread.
Use the leaders of the top bar of knots to
outline the bottom of this. These are the
leaders of the 3 bars of knots in the diamond,
which the half hitches will make.
Close the diamond at the bottom with an
overhand knot around the outline leader
threads and leave the 2 threads to one side
for the moment.
Finish off the 4 threads on either side with
a very tight overhand knot and cut them very
close.
There are 4 motifs of this type separated by
3 V shapes.

2nd motif: Take as leader the thread nearest
the 1st motif. Knot above in half hitches the
2 threads after it. Take as leader the knotting
thread of the 2nd half hitch and work above
with the 2 threads which are next in line.
Start again on a 3rd line.
Reproduce the 2nd half of the motif
symmetrically and finish the V by an overhand knot with the 2 core threads. Work an
overhand knot with the 4 other threads,
pulling it tight against the half hitches, and
cut them close. Work similar overhand knots
with the threads which are still free under
the double knot bars delineating the 2 ends
of the loop, with the exception of the last
thread and the leader of this row of knotting.

Design: Marie-Jeanine SOLVIT

Use these to make a series of 12 knots in a single knotted chain. After the last knot in the chain, make an overhand knot on the thread and cut the end close. Bring other thread of this chain up to join the holding cord. Join them with an overhand knot. The loop thus formed is used to hook the tie-back to the wall behind the curtain.

You will see that 2 threads still remain free beneath each of the 7 motifs of the tie-back. Thread a bead onto the bottom of each motif and keep it in place with an overhand knot. Cut off the surplus string.

The braid shown in the photograph is made of the same type of string. It is a simple braid of 3 pairs of threads which you can use as another type of tie-back or to add a finishing touch to hide any nails, tacks or seam lines that may be obvious on a textile wall covering. Allow twice the required length of the finished work when you cut your threads. Make all the vertical strips first and finish with the horizontals, covering up all the ends. This hand-made braid fits snugly around the contour of rounded as well as right-angled shapes. You may also decorate your braid, perhaps with beads matching those on the tie-back, or with clusters of overhand knots, or with circles of string coiled up flat. Glue the braid in position, also using headless nails, just partially driven in, to keep it taut while the glue dries. Pull out the nails after the glue has completely dried.

25

Hanging garden

During the day, this hanging garden will
bring life and color into your room.
In the evening, its glow
will create a warm and pleasant atmosphere.
It is easy to make.

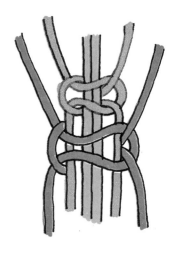

The pyramid technique:
the threads of each knot
are included in the
following flat knot.

Materials

163 m (180 yd) of rust wool
12 large olive green ceramic beads
1 bell-shaped lampshade frame which flares
out at the bottom, about 14 cm (6 in.) high,
with base ring 20 cm (8 in.) in diameter, a
top ring about 11 cm (4 in.) in diameter,
the electrical materials necessary for the
lighting — an electric light socket, electric
cord, an electric plug (unless you already
have a ceiling fitting)
1 plastic bracelet (ring) about 8 cm (3 in.)
in diameter
1 bowl about 40 cm (16 in.) in diameter for
the plants

Method

Prepare 12 pieces of wool 5.30 m (6 yd)
long, 6 pieces 4.50 m (5 yd) long, 12 pieces
4.40 m (4¾ yd) long, 6 pieces 24 cm (9½ in.)
long, and finally 1 piece 3.50 m (3¾ yd) long.
Double over the 12 longest pieces and, with
the 3.50 m (3¾ yd) piece, make a handle to
hang them by, following the instructions
given for the handle of the ornamental
hanger on page 36.
This handle will be 12 cm (4¾ in.) high

overall, 2 cm (¾ in.) of this being the stem
and 10 cm (4 in.) the oval ring above.
Work 5 rows of alternating flat knots, then
knot your threads in half hitches onto the
plastic bracelet (ring), so that they form a
circle of horizontal double knots over it.
Above this knotting, add the 4.50 m (5 yd)
lengths, mounted so that they straddle the
flat knots of the row before last and pass in
front of the knotting without being knotted
onto it. Use these threads to make 4
alternate vertical half hitches (2 each) on 1
core thread coming from the cording on the
bracelet.
With the 3 threads remaining between each
group of these vertical braids, make 2 flat
knots and a half flat knot.
Now add the 4.40 m (4¾ yd) lengths using
to the bracelet using reverse lark's head
knots, in such a way that you insert each
length on either side of the braids of 2 flat
knots and a half flat knot. Make these last
threads add into a single knotted chain of
5 knots. Use the threads of this knotted
chain as the knotting threads of a line of
flat knots with 3 core threads, followed by
another staggered row, leaving 1 thread free
between each flat knot. Use the threads
lying to the right and left of this free thread
to make 4 alternate vertical half hitches over

it on the following row. Then, taking as
leader threads the core threads of 1 flat knot
out of 2, work bars of diagonal double knots
with 4 knotting threads over each.
Bring the leader threads together again with
an overhand knot. Then thread 1 green bead
onto the threads lying in the middle of these
inverted V's and continue with the diagonal
double knot bars to form diamond shapes
with a green bead in the middle of each.
Leave this part of the work for the moment
while you cover the lampshade frame with
rust wool, using what remains of the cut
lengths for winding around all the metal struts.
Slip the lampshade frame into the work and
hold it in position with pins pushed through
the top of the frame, so that the bottom of
it lies level with the point where the leader
threads of the diamond shapes meet up.
Pass these threads over the front edge of the
frame, wind them around it and bring them
back to the front so as to attach the base of
each diamond shape to the frame. These
leader threads will then become the core
threads of flat knots. The knotting threads
of the flat knots so positioned make 1 large
flat knot with 6 core threads which are
inserted in the middle between the beaded
diamond shapes. Now use the threads next to
the whole flat knot of the preceding row. This

gives a pyramid of 7 flat knots of which the last has 18 core threads. This motif, repeated 3 times around the work, divides all the knotting threads into 3 quite separate braids. The small section of the frame will still be visible between these threads which have been drawn apart from each other. Mount on each, in the usual way, 2 pieces of wool 24 cm (9½ in.) long. Wrap a small piece of adhesive tape around the ends of the 4 strands of wool so that you can thread them together through a green bead. (If your beads have fairly small holes, as the ones shown here did, you can only hold them in place by the pressure of the wool. If your beads have big holes, retain them with an overhand knot. In either case, leave a 4-5 cm (1½-2 in.) pom-pon tail.)

Thread a bead onto the pair of threads marking the middle of the last large flat knots. Then, on either side, make a flat knot with 4 core threads and 2 knotting threads. Three sets of 8 threads remain: make each into a flat knot with 6 core threads. Continue with 3 braids of flat knots spaced out as follows: 2 cm (¾ in.) (3 times), 2.5 cm (1 in.) (twice), 3 cm (1¼ in.) (twice). Join the outer thread of each motif of the adjacent motif with an overhand knot 10 cm (4 in.) from the last flat knot. Take 1 of the motifs with 3 braids: after knotting the outer threads to the adjacent one as described, take the 2nd thread as leader thread of a bar of diagonal double knots on which the 4 threads of the lateral braid and 2 lateral threads of the central braid will be worked. In the following row, leave the 1st 3 threads free. Take the 4th as leader thread of a row of knotting alongside the previous one, on which you work 5 threads. Leave 2 threads free under the last row of knotting and take the 3rd as leader thread of a bar of diagonal double knots with 3 knotting threads. The leader threads join up again in the middle. Use the 1 on the left to make 2 half hitches over the 1 on the right. This point marks the middle of the motif which you complete by working the instructions in reverse order. All that remains is to make an enormous overhand knot with all the threads, about 12 cm (4¾ in.) below the last knot. Put the electric cord through the top. Attach a socket, and select a light bulb of not more than 60 watts so that it will not overheat the plant which you put in the round bowl.

Because of the weight of the plant and wet earth, you must hang this garden from a fairly solid beam.

Use a low watt light bulb. Bright lights get very hot and can cause fire.

Design:
Marie-Jeanine SOLVIT

Bead purse

A combination of beads and flat knots created this purse.

Mounting threads on
the ring. The blue
threads are the core
threads of the flat knots.

Design:
Marie-Jeanine SOLVIT

·Threads mounted on the ring thread bearer. The blue threads are the core threads of the flat knots. This small item is easy to make.

Materials

A small curtain or belt ring
36 russet-colored oval wooden beads 1 cm (¼ in.) long
1 ball of very fine natural colored wool.

Method

Mount 12 pieces of wool 1.60 m (1¾ yd) long on the ring. Work 1st row of 6 flat knots. In the following row, add 2 pieces 1.50 m (1½ yd) long between each of the staggered flat knots. Do the same on the following row using threads of the same length. You now have a row of 24 flat knots.* Pass the core threads of every 3rd knot through a bead, then separate these 8 beads with 3 rows of alternating flat knots. Continue with the flat knots for 2 more rows.*
Repeat * to * twice more, staggering the beads.
Now separate the work into 8 groups of threads. Starting from the right, make a leaf with each of these groups using 3 parallel bars of double knots running diagonally from right to left. At the left-hand side, knot each row onto the leader of the following row.
Thread a bead onto the last 2 remaining threads and finish off by making an overhand knot covered by a 2nd knot to give it more body.
The drawstrings are 4 pieces of wool 50 cm (20 in.) long threaded in pairs at regular intervals between the flat knots of the 3rd row of the last group of 5.
Two come out at the right after being threaded all the way around the purse. The other 2 do the same on the left. Finish off with an overhand knot over 4 threads. Add 2 beads to each drawstring, with 2 threads through each and make a final overhand knot to hold each 2 in place.
Do not thread the drawstrings through the knots themselves, as they must be able to slip easily past each other.
This project is easier to do if you use the bottom of a jar as a shape to work around.

Leisure bag

*This is a very attractive bag for leisure wear.
It has a separate pocket on the front
where you can keep your wallet,
the cord which keeps the pocket closed
will hold a newspaper or magazine.*

Materials

2 wooden handles (available from some
large department stores, crafts and sewing
supply shops
16 pale blue ceramic beads
252 m (277 yd) natural macramé cotton cut
into 72 pieces 3.50 m (3¾ yd) long
37 m (40 yd) dark beige cotton cut into
13 pieces 1.50 m (1½ yd) long; 19 pieces
0.35 m (2/5 yd) long; 1 piece 0.60 m (¾ yd)
long for threading the beads along the bottom;
1 piece 0.50 m (½ yd) long for the mounting
thread of the pocket; 2 pieces 0.30 m (12 in.)
long for the 2 beads on the pocket.

Method

Mount 36 pieces of natural cotton on each
wooden handle, alternating a single reverse
lark's head knot with a double one (see
page 20). This gives you 6 threads wound
around for every 4 working threads.
Make a row of 18 flat knots, then take as
leader threads for a bar of diagonal double
knots the threads: 12, 24, 36, 48, 60 and 72.
Work very steep bars of knots, right to left.

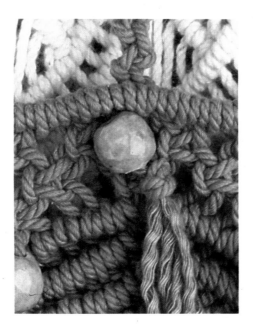

Design: Marie-Jeanine SOLVIT

curving the leader thread so that it is slightly
convex. When all the threads are knotted, then
use the 1st free thread on the right as leader
thread, curving away as you make another
row so that it is slightly concave. This forms a
long leaf shape. Now use the 6th thread,
counting from right to left, as the leader of a
bar of double knots left to right, followed by
a 2nd row to produce the same leaf design
in the opposite direction from the 1st.
Cover the leader thread of the last bar of
double knots on the right of each half of
the work by the knotting of 5 threads, then
by the 1st 6 free threads on the left of the
other half of the work. This is the way you
join the sides of the bag.
Continue working in this way until you have
7 successive leaves down the length. Finish
with a row of flat knots. Then turn the bag
outside in and, using overhand knots, tie the
threads together in pairs, taking 1 thread from
each side of the bag each time.
Turn the right side out again and tie the
0.50 m (½ yd) length of beige cotton to the
bag at the bottom of the 2nd row of leaves
from the top, to the left of the 2nd and to
the right of the 5th. Mount on it 12 pieces of
beige cotton 1.50 m (1½ yd) long using double
reverse lark's head knots. Work 2 rows of

alternating flat knots, then 1 flat knot under the 2nd knot and 1 under the 5th of the preceding row. Now use the 1st thread on the left and the thread on the right of the middle of the central flat knot to make a diagonal bar of double knots, from left to right, covered by 5 knotting threads. Use the symmetrically opposite thread to make bars of double knots from right to left.

Now thread 30 cm (12 in.) beige lengths through the loop of each of the flat knots on the 3rd row and thread a bead through it, holding it in place with an overhand knot over 2 threads. Work a 2nd row of bars of double knots, up against the preceding bars, crossing over the threads in the middle. Work a 3rd row making a flat knot with the leader threads and using as core threads those which are hanging beneath the 2 beads. Work a 4th bar of double knots on the middle threads only, again crossing over the threads in the middle, and accentuate this by a 5th row with 2 knotting threads and a 6th with a single knotting thread.

Start the last bar of double knots from the edge and go right down to the middle of the pocket. Over it, knot 12 threads and join the leader threads together with an overhand knot in the middle. Thread a bead onto each, and secure with an overhand knot. Make an overhand knot on every thread 5 cm (2 in.) from the last bar of knotting. Leave a short length of fringe, then cut and unravel the cotton.

Mount the last 1.50 m (1½ yd) length of beige cotton centrally on the working already at the top of the bag and make a single knotted chain of 24 knots. Thread a bead onto 1 of the 2 threads and tie them together with an overhand knot. Trim the threads, leaving a little fringe, and unravel them like the others.

Slip the bead on this chain through the hole in the middle of the top of the pocket to close it and enable you to keep a newspaper behind the chain cord.

Using a fine crochet hook, thread a 0.60 m (¾ yd) length of beige cotton in and out at the bottom of the bag, inserting 11 beads as you go. Secure this thread at either end with an overhand knot, leaving a fringe the same length as the fringes you will put between the beads, using for these the 19 pieces 0.3 m (2/5 yd) long. Unravel them in the same way as the other fringes.

Strengthen the sides and bottom of the bag by stitching with invisible thread.

It is best to line this bag so that you can carry small items which might otherwise slip through the mesh.

1920s belt with giant buckle

You need a slim waist to wear this belt.
The large central motif
makes this project very unusual.

Materials

40 m (44 yd) pink macramé cotton cut into
7 pieces 5.60 m (6 yd) long
1 ceramic buckle 12 cm (4¾ in.) diameter
with 2 holes 3 cm (1¼ in.) apart at each side.

Method

Thread each end of 1 of the lengths of cotton
through from the back of the ceramic buckle
to the front. Cross the ends over so that they
serve as a double holding thread on which
you mount the 6 other lengths in reverse
lark's head knots.
With threads 1 and 14 as 1st leaders, make 6
V-shaped bars of diagonal double knots, then
* 2 braids of 4 flat knots and a half flat knot,
3 bars of diagonal double knots with the
point in the opposite direction from the
preceding V, 1 flat knot with 4 core threads
and 2 knotting threads on either side, and 3
diagonal bars of double knots in a V,
symmetrical with the preceding ones. *
Repeat from * to * 3 times.
Continue with 2 braids of 4 flat knots and a
half flat knot, followed by 9 V-shaped
diagonal bars of double knots pointing
towards the flat knots.
Finish off with 2 horizontal bars of double
knots, using as leaders the 2 outer threads
which turn at either end between the 2 bars
of knotting, then emerge at either end of the
2nd bar of knotting. Thread these through
the holes onto the reverse side of the round
ceramic buckle.

Design: Maryse DUBOULOIS

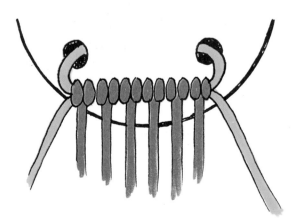

When mounting threads
on to the holding cord,
cross them over to form
a double thread.

Decorative design for a plain door

*An original version of
an old-fashioned door decoration.*

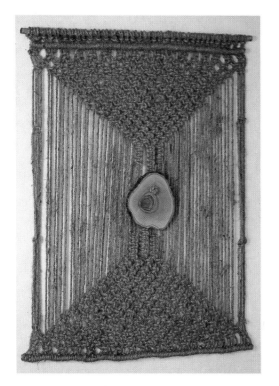

The interior design of modern homes is
extremely bare. But you can decorate dreary,
mass-produced flush doors yourself. The
door opposite is a new version of an old style.

Materials

313 m (346 yd) jute or sisal cut into: 56
pieces 4 m (4½ yd) long; 12 pieces 4.60 m
(5 yd) long; 34 pieces 1 m (1 yd) long.
4 small wooden plaques, for example, or a
round section of 5 m (5.1/3 yd) rope approx.
1 cm (¼ in.) diam. cut into 6 pieces 70 cm
(28 in.) long
2 pieces of narrow dowelling or thin bamboo
approx. 80 cm (32 in.) long
1 box wooden beads and some nails.

Method

Panel for the top of the door Take
28 pieces of jute or sisal 4 m (4½ yd)
long, 6 pieces 4.60 m (5 yd) long, 2
pieces of rope, and 1 wooden plaque.
Pierce a hole in the middle of the
plaque large enough for you to thread
two pieces of string through and back
again, after you have made an overhand
knot to keep the wood in place (see
below).
Mount the threads on one of the pieces
of dowelling or bamboo in this order:
14 pieces 4 m (4½ yd) long, 6 pieces
4.60 (5 yd) long, 14 pieces 4 m (4½ yd)
long.
Using a piece of rope as thread bearer,
work a horizontal bar of double knots to
accentuate the start.
Then, work 17 flat knots. Continue
in rows of alternating flat knots,
decreasing one knot at either end of
each row until the 15th row, where you
will be left with three flat knots in the
middle. Work three vertical braids on
these 12 threads, the first of 4 flat
knots, the second - the middle of the
work - of 7 flat knots, the third of 4
flat knots. It is at this point that you
attach the plaque of wood by threading
the 2 core threads of the central flat knot
from the back to the front, through
the hole pierced in the middle of the
wood. Pull the ends through with a
fine crochet hook.
After making an overhand knot on
these 2 threads, thread them through
to the back of the wood again. (The
hole should be only just large enough
for the threads, so that the string knot
will not slip through.)
Next, reproduce the above motif
symmetrically, beginning with the 7
flat knots of the central braid below the

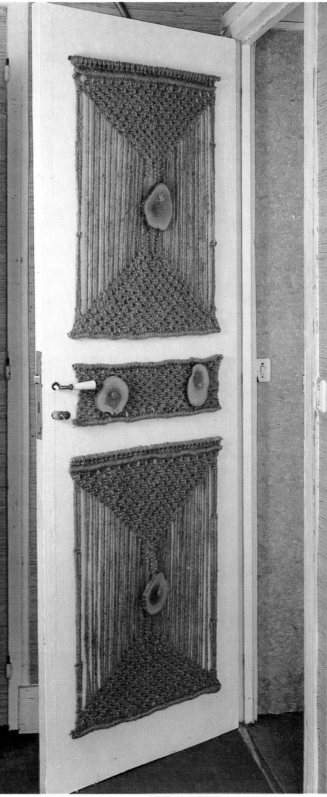

Design: Marie-Jeanine SOLVIT

bottom edge of the round piece of wood.
On the 13th row of the alternating
flat knots, use the four threads at
either side of the top of the panel
to make one flat knot in line with the
third row from the top of the motif,
then one flat knot 14 cm (5½ in.)
lower down, another 30 cm (12 in.)
below that, then a final knot lined up
with the 13th row from the bottom
of the motif. Finish the 14th and 15th
rows by using all available threads in
the normal way.
After the 15th row work a bar of
horizontal double knots on a length
of rope, like that used at the start.
Glue the rope and jute together with
transparent glue at each end.

Lower panel This is identical with the
upper panel.

Middle panel Mounted on a piece of
rope, the 34 pieces of jute 1 m (1 yd)
long will be made up into a first row
of 17 flat knots followed by 9
alternating rows of flat knots.
Finish the bottom in the same way as
the large panels. The two remaining
circles of wood are tied in position
about 5 cm (2 in.) from the sides of
the panel, and this completes the work.
All that remains to be done is to fix
the three panels on the door. Thread
each of the nails through a bead and
hammer it in carefully so as not to
break the bead.
You must stretch the sides of the
three panels as much as possible both
length- and width-wise, so that the
edges lie in perfectly straight lines.
As the end of the jute has been glued
on to the rope with transparent glue,
the rope may be trimmed close after
the glue has completely dried.

Ornamental hanging for a large tray and three baskets

A hanging with an exotic holiday air.
It also makes an attractive dumb waiter.

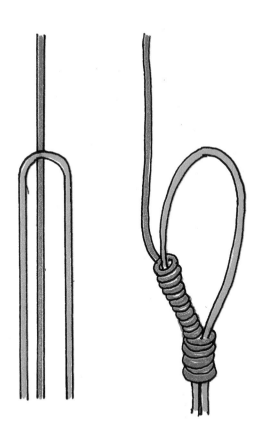

Hanging loop

Materials

1 times 10 m (11 yd) x 2
3 times 4 m (4½ yd) x 2
4 times 2.50 m (2¾ yd) x 2
for each third of the work, that is:
3 times 33 m (36½ yd) of natural macramé
cotton = 99 m (110 yd). To this, add 3
threads, about 2.80 m (3 yd) each, to make
the loops to hang it by. So allow 107.5 m
(120 yd) in all. 1 big tray + 3 baskets. Each
third of the work includes a loop to hang it
up by.

Hanging loop

Let us call the thread which will form the
loop A (see diagram). Form a loop with 8
threads, then 12 cm (4¾ in.) from the top,
attach the thread A with a loop and wind it
round the 8 threads going towards the top,
simply coiling it round without knotting for
about 2 or 3 cm (1 in.)
Then divide the work in two, so that the
thread A can be wound up round the loop and
down again to meet up with the 3 cm (1 in.)
wound round about at the beginning. Tie an
overhand knot with what remains of thread
A. The threads are now ready to be worked
in half flat knots for 90 cm (36 in.) This will
form a twisted braid round 6 core threads.
Now, add to each group of 2 threads coming
from the center of this twisted braid, 2

threads which will be used to make the flat
knots and the three new twisted braids of
half flat knots.
The 3 twisted braids are 32 cm (12 in.) long.
Each then breaks up into 2 twisted braids
of double knotted chain with 2 lengths 12 cm
(6 in.) long, making 6 twisted braids of
double knotted chain, tied 2 by 2 at the
bottom with a flat knot of 4 threads (2 in
the middle, 2 at the side). After 8 cm (3 in.)
of taut single threads, make a final pom-pon
fringe, with two rows of staggered flat knots,
and finish by untwisting the threads to
complete the tail of the pom-pon.
For the rest of it: to the two remaining
groups of 2 threads coming out from the
bottom of the first long twisted braid above,
add one double length to each and make two
braids in flat knots, 26 cm (10½ in.) long.
When it gets to this length, cross over the
two twisted braids made in this way with a
single flat knot of 2 lateral threads and 4 core
threads and continue the two twisted braids
of flat knots till they are 12 cm (4¾ in.) long.
When the three parts of the hanging have
reached this stage, bring the 6 final braids
of flat knots together with two rows of
staggered flat knots. These will form the body
of a large pom-pon, bound round in the
middle, and under which hang all the threads
which you unwind to form the 20 cm (8 in.)
long skirt of the pom-pon.
Now place the central tray and the three
baskets in their supports, wedging them well in.

Design:
Marie-Jeanine SOLVIT

37

Rainbow hammock

Now you can float on a rainbow.
This colorful hammock will
light up any garden.

Materials

2 bright red broom handles
About 45 m (50 yd) of dyed sisal or synthetic
macramé fibre (I found the gradation of
colors I wanted by mixing the two) in each
of the following colors: violet, royal blue
(2 balls of this color), bright blue, dark green,
deep moss green, lime green, bright light
green, lemon yellow, light honey yellow,
deep honey yellow, bright orange, orange-red,
light red and deep red.
400 m natural macramé cotton 3 mm (1/8 in.)
diameter cut into: 6 pieces 15 m (16½ yd)
long for the center of the hammock,
528 pieces 50 cm (20 in.) long for the pom-
pons round the edge, 2 pieces 5 m (5½ yd)
long for the side supports and 2 lengths of
9 m (10 yd) for the loops.

Method

Mount on one of the broom handles a 15 m
(16 ½ yd) length of each of the colors in the
order given above, then the 6 lengths of
natural cotton for the center, and then a
second length of each of the colors in reverse
order.
Mount them all using double reverse lark's
head knots (see p. 20). Work in 5 rows in
alternating flat knots, then leave 5 cm (2 in.)
of thread free before working another five
rows. Repeat this until the hammock is at
least 2 m (2¼ yd) long, then attach the ends
to the second broom handle.
To do this, place the wood horizontally straight

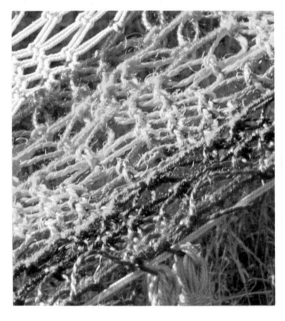

onto a wall or work surface and hammer in a
large nail placed centrally 75 cm (30 in.)
above. Take up each thread, in the order in

which they lie, and roll it three times round
the broom handle. Then lift it up over the
nail and down again to the opposite end of
the broom handle and wind it round. Do the
same in the opposite direction with the
thread symmetrical to it. Each time you have
two threads wound round in each direction,
finish them off with an overhand knot and
cut them, leaving a tail. Do the same with all
the threads. They will form a triangle which
will get narrower and narrower towards the
natural colored center of the hammock.
These center threads play no part in this
'spider' formation. Bind a matching natural
thread 14 times round the wood on either
side of this central section so as to keep a
space between it and the 'spider'.
You now need a 9 m (10 yd) length of natural
cotton to make the loop to hang the
hammock up by (16 cm (6½ in.) long overall,
3 cm (1¼ in.) for the base and 13 cm (5¼ in.)
for the loop) following the instructions given
for the loop on page 36. Make the 'spider'
at the other end of the hammock by setting
threads 2.25 m (2½ yd) long on the wooden
handle used for mounting the original threads,
in reverse lark's head knots on one side and
the overhand knot made with every two
threads on the opposite side.
Along the sides of the hammock use border
loops. These loops are smaller at the end of
the sections of 5 alternating flat knots. Each
of these is used to insert a pom-pon
consisting of 12 lengths of 50 cm (20 in.)
long natural cotton. Make the tie round the
pom-pon with the colored threads, keeping
to the order of the graded shades.

Design: Marie-Jeanine SOLVIT

I used 1.50 m (1¾ yd) lengths for these ties, and let the starting and finishing threads hang with those of the pom-pon. I split the length of the side of the hammock into two, so that I ended up with dark red in the center; I continued towards the other end of the hammock, symmetrically grading the shades once again. Wind each colored tie round 6 times to form the pom-pon. Twist the threads of the spider round on themselves for a multi-colored hanger. Then make a big pom-pon, using the 8 natural threads left after attaching the center threads on the second handle, and the binding made on either side to keep the dark red threads apart — as on the other end.

Finally strengthen the sides by threading a double thread of natural cotton through the border loops, stretching it slightly lengthways, and knotting it at either end. Don't forget to cut the wood 105 cm (42 in.) long.

Decorated box

*For sewing, photos, letters, cigarettes
and almost anything.
This square box was once a biscuit container.*

Materials

1 biscuit box 21 x 21 cm (about 8 x 8 in.)
1 ball of thin parcel string.
3.20 m (3½ yd) of thicker parcel string.
33 orange wooden beads
A little transparent glue
Light beige adhesive cloth to cover the box.
These instructions match the drawing on the
left. The lid of the box in the photograph on
page 41 is the other way up.

Method

Mount thirty lengths of thin string, each
1.70 m (2 yd) in double reverse lark's head
knots on the thick string thread bearer,
leaving a 12 cm (4¾ in.) of this thick string
free to the left of the work.
Pin this first thread bearer row on to a sheet
of white paper, attached to your knotting
board, on which you have reproduced the
design shown here, making it bigger to fit the
square box. Follow the lines (preferably
drawn with a thick soft tip pen) with the
thick string, which will be the leader thread

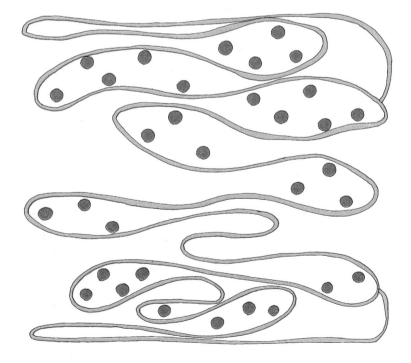

Design: Marie-Jeanine SOLVIT

of this series of undulating rows of knotting. For a project of this size, it is pointless to shorten the threads by bundling them, as you are then able to thread on the beads as you go. Secure the turns of your rows of knotting firmly with pins so that you don't over-run the size limit set by the surface area of the lid of the tin. As you work, thread on the beads, and keep those of them which have to be held in position near the bar of knotting above with an overhand knot underneath the bead.

Thread on the beads just before doing the double knots on the bar of knotting directly below where the bead is to go. The last horizontal row of knotting is continued to curve back up around the lower left-hand corner.

After you have completed the pattern, work the first thread at the top on the left of the thread bearer on the short length of thick string you left to form a corner at the top left-hand side of the work.

Finish off all the threads under the bottom horizontal bar of knotting with overhand knots. Then attach the whole macramé work to the cloth covered lid of the box with transparent glue.

Three-color wall decoration

*This simple, attractive composition is
decorated with circles and rods, made of
garnet, beige and orange sisal string.*

Design: Maryse DUBOULOIS

Materials

34 m (37½ yd) garnet sisal 5 mm (¼ in.)
diameter.
51 m (56 yd) orange sisal 5 mm (¼ in.)
diameter.
184 m (202 yd) light brown sisal 3 mm
(3/16 in.) diameter.
1 length of dowelling 48 cm (19 in.) long
by 1 cm (3/8 in.) diameter.
2 lengths of dowelling 34 cm (13½ in.) long
by 1 cm (3/8 in.) diameter.
1 length of dowelling 64 cm (25 in.) long
by 1 cm (3/8 in.) diameter.
1 length of dowelling 60 cm (24 in.) long by
2 cm (¾ in.) diameter.
4 wooden curtain rings.

Method

On the 48 cm (19 in.) length of dowelling,
mount in double reverse lark's head knots:
4 lengths of garnet, each 8.50 m (9½ yd) long.
12 lengths of brown, each 8.50 m (9½ yd)
long.

6 lengths of orange, each 8.50 m (9½ yd) long. On an inserted leader thread, work one row of horizontal double knot bars. Then, 6 cm (2½ in.) lower down, arrange 4 brown lengths, each 12.80 m (14 yd) long, so that you have a 4-thread leader for one bar of horizontal knotting, followed by a second in which 8 threads cross over one another. Make the 4 ends emerging on the left into a 22 cm (8¾ in.) long spiral braid of half flat knots, the 4 threads emerging on the right are made up into a similar 12 cm (4¾ in.) spiral braid.

Mount another leader for a row of horizontal knotting consisting of 4 lengths, each 8 m (9 yd) long, and work a 30 cm (12 in.) spiral braid in half flat knots to the left of the row of knotting, and to the right a 15 cm (6 in.) spiral braid in the same knots. Leave the 4 brown spiral braids on one side for the moment to work with threads 17, 18, 19, 20, 21, 22, 23, 24, 25, 26, 27, 28, 29, 30, 31 and 32 a double bar of horizontal knotting, rounded at the ends, on a leader of 4 inserted threads.

Cover a ring below with threads 23, 24, 25, 26, 27, 28 and 29; wind the 2 threads at the side around the wooden ring to hide it completely, at each side, before trimming up the half hitches at its base again. Level with the bottom of the central double row of horizontal double knots, cover a ring with the threads 6, 7, 8, 9, 10, 11, 12. Take up the 4 threads emerging from the ends of the double row of horizontal knotting and work, on the left, a spiral braid 15 cm (6 in.) long, in half flat knots, and on the right 7 cm (3 in.) long in the same knot.

Go back to the 1st spiral of half flat knots left at the top-right of the work. Use its 4 threads as leaders of a diagonal row of double knots, worked from right to left on all the orange threads plus 12 brown threads. Use the 4 threads from the 2nd spiral braid of half flat knots as the leaders of a bar of knotting, 1st horizontal, then diagonal, beginning 7 cm (3 in.) below the start of the 1st.

Starting from the right, make 3 braids of orange flat knots as follows: 7 and a half flat knot, 7 and a half flat knot, and 6 and a half flat knot. Then make 3 braids of brown flat knots: 8 and a half flat knot, 5 and a half flat knot, and 2 and a half flat knot. On the left, 8 brown threads hang free.

Work all these 32 threads into a horizontal row of knotting, using as thread bearer a 34 cm (13½ in.) length of dowelling.

The 4 threads on the left of this dowel then become leaders of a horizontal row of knotting. Then, still on the left, the 1st 4

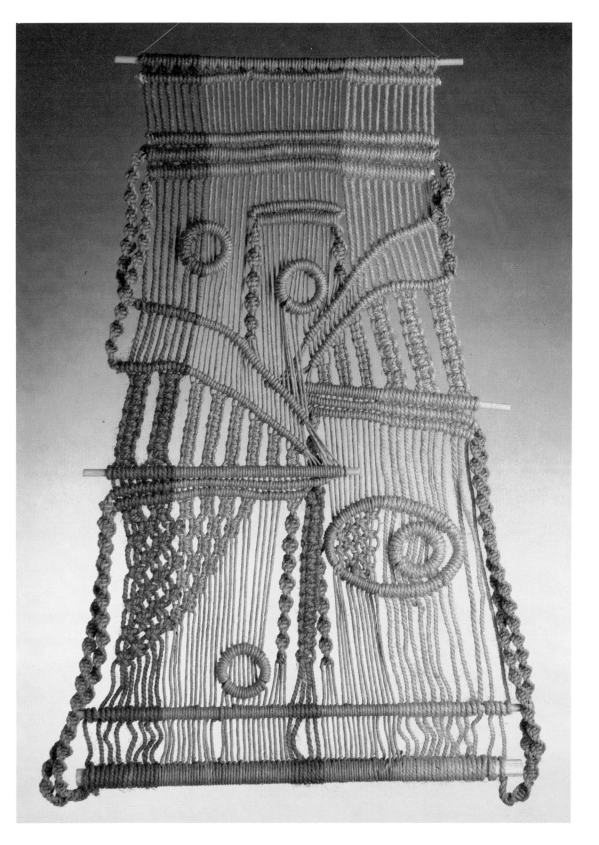

threads form the leader of a 2nd horizontal row of knotting, underneath the 1st. The leaders of the 1st row of knotting are made up into a 48 cm (19 in.) spiral braid of half flat knots on the right. These leaders of the 2nd row into a spiral braid of the same length.

About 9 cm (3½ in.) from this 2nd horizontal bar of knotting, make an oval shape with 8 added leader threads, on which you work all the threads except the last 3 orange threads on the right and the 1st 4 on the left. Inside this oval, work the brown threads in alternating flat knots and put in a ring, round which you work the 6 orange threads on the right. The 4 free threads on the left of the oval are made up into a 34 cm (13½ in.) spiral braid of half flat knots. Return to the left-hand half of the work. Work two bars of knots using as leaders the 4 threads from the spiral braids on the left, laid out as the photo shows, into a left to right diagonal and starting off 7 cm (3 in.) apart. Follow these with braids of flat knots. From left to right: 2 times 7 garnet flat knots, then: 10, 9, 7 flat knots and a half flat knot, 6, 4 and 2 brown knots. A row of horizontal knotting on a 34 cm (13½ in.) length of dowelling. The two following bars of knotting will have for leaders the first 4 threads on the right. On the passage of the threads laid towards the right on the 2nd horizontal row of knots, mount 2 garnet lengths of 2.80 m (3 yd) and make a braid of 13 flat knots.

Then, with the first 4 brown threads on the right, make a 21 cm (8 in.) spiral cord of half flat knots.

Leave 4 threads free, then make 4 braids of 2 flat knots, followed by braids of 2 alternating flat knots, thus: 3, 3, 2, 2, 1, 1. The garnet threads are worked in alternating flat knots, which, at the bottom, follow the slant of the neighbouring brown knots. Insert a ring and work round it the 9 brown threads lying to the left of the vertical brown spiral cord. Now cord all threads on to the 64 x 1 cm (32 x 3/8 in.) dowelling rod. The cord on to the 60 x 2 cm (30 x ¾ in.) rod, about 7 cm down.

The 2 lateral brown spiral cords merge into one with 6 core threads and 2 knotting threads, 7 cm (3 in.) long on the right and 5 cm (2 in.) on the left. Cut 2 core threads and finish off the knotting threads. Each has 4 threads left. These will cross over each other to be the leaders of a last horizontal double knot bar, over which the threads will all be knotted. Then finish off the threads with transparent glue and cut close.

Clôche lampshade

This is made in natural macramé cotton. It looks pretty and fits in with many styles of interior decoration.

Materials

1 hemispherical lampshade frame 25 cm (10 in.) high with 40 cm (16 in.) diameter at the base, 9 cm (3½ in.) at the top. 370 m (407 yd) of macramé cotton (1/8 in.) diameter.

Method

Mount 30 lengths of 4.50 m (5 yd) on the top ring and make a first diagonal double knot bar covered by 3 knotting threads, then straddle a thread over each end.
Then work flat knots in the points of these bars of knotting, and start off again with the

Design: Maryse DUBOULOIS

diagonal bars of knotting, adding a new thread at the beginning of each.

Before forming a diamond shape, make a trellis (see the glossary) with 5 criss-crossing threads, then return, while working diagonal rows of knotting, to delineate the diamonds of this section, adding one thread at each end of the bars of knots.

Next come 2 rows of staggered flat knots. Again you add a thread to those under the points where the preceding bars of knots meet (one on each row of flat knots). Once again, work bars of diagonal knots,

parallel to the preceding ones, adding a thread to each.

Leave 4 threads free on either side of the points formed in this way at the top, and again work diagonal double knot bars to form a small diamond round these taut free threads. Once more, add a thread to each and continue working them until diamond shapes are formed, into which the points of the bars of knotting from the previous section dip down. Fill out these diamonds with large flat knots work 8 core threads and 4 knotting threads.

Next work your threads into a trellis with 9 threads criss-crossing, then close up the diamonds with diagonal double knot bars, under which lie 3 rows of staggered flat knots, outlined below by a last row of bars of knotting, which finish at the bottom metal ring of the lampshade on either side of a flat knot. Pull your threads tight to work a bar of horizontal knots round the bottom ring of the lampshade and cut off, leaving a length of fringe as shown in the photograph. Don't use a very high powered electric light bulb. Bright lights get very hot and can cause a fire.

Fancy cushion

*A pink design on a white background
framed in a black oval, gives this cushion
an early nineteenth-century look.*

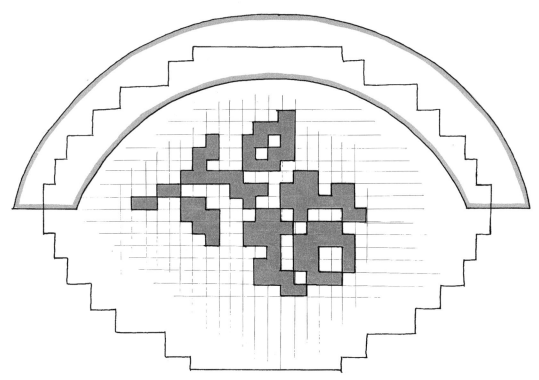

Draw a grid of the white background and mark out the
motif, which is done in Cavandoli work. The blue outline
shows the shape of the background and how to appliqué
it to the white surface.

Materials

47 lengths of black rug wool, each 1 m (1 yd)
long and 8 m (9 yd) for the leader threads:
55 m (56 yd) in all.
1 ball of pink rug wool.
36 lengths of thick white cotton, 2 m (2 yd)
long + 6.50 m (7 yd) for the leader thread:
i.e. 78.50 (79 yd) in all.
1 ball of black silk thread.
1 piece of black fabric 45 x 35 cm (18 x
14 in.) for the lining.

Method

Follow the diagram, taking 1 square to
represent 1 half hitch (that is, 2 threads side
by side). Reproduce the pink design on a
white cotton base, using Cavandoli stitch,
which involves working in 2 colors: one for

Design: Odile TRENTESAUX

the bottom, the other for the motif design. Work the background in rows of horizontal knotting and the motif in vertical knotting. This technique calls for tightly-worked knots and allows you to reproduce designs which resemble embroidery worked in cross-stitch, each square of the design being one knot in a bar of vertical knots. The diagram defines the edge of the white background, the circumference of which is cut out in steps.

These will disappear when you lay out the black leader thread for the oval frame. Extend the squares of the diagram for the black frame, and pin your work in black wool round the pink.

Work the 47 threads mounted on the first leader thread into a first row of knotting, then a second, 1.5 cm (¾ in.) from the first. There follow 5 bars of knotting, on which here and there you add some half-hitches as

the work spreads out. Sew the threads in behind the last row and hide them with the black fabric oval lining.

Now go back to the threads which separate the first two bars of knotting and work over them in vertical half-hitches with the black silk. Sew black oval border round the white background with invisible thread. Line the macramé.

All you have to do now is to stuff the cushion.

Christmas tree

Heating often has a drying effect on real pine trees,
but it will not affect the freshness of this tree
which will last for years
and shed no needles.
Even when it is stripped of its tinsel accessories,
this tree can decorate some corner of your home.

Materials

1 broom handle cut to 1 m (1 yd) long.
1 ring 2.5 cm (1 in.) diameter.
1 round section of wood with the center cut out (into which you fit the trunk).
6 lampshade rings: 10, 18, 24, 30, 38 and 50 cm (4, 7, 9½, 12, 15, and 20 in.) in diameter.
4 balls of dark green wool.
7 balls of medium green wool.
4 balls of light green wool.

Method

Hammer a long nail vertically into the top of the broom handle. Hang the 6 lamp rings, using 4 light green threads, knotted onto the nail and knotted an equal distance apart onto the circumference of each ring, beginning with the lowest one. Position the rings, respectively, the following distance from the top: 87, 74, 60, 47, 36 and 20 cm (36, 29½, 24, 19, 14½ and 8 in.).
1st section. Mount, in lark's head knots on the last but one circle from the bottom, 164

dark green lengths, each 1.50 m (1¼ yd). Double them up, attaching on two at a time. Work 2 rows of alternating flat knots, without pulling the wool too tight (4 core threads, 2 knotting threads from each side). Then a third row of alternating flat knots, working it half way between the two metal rings. Again, 2 rows of alternating flat knots just above the bottom ring. Divide up the threads into groups of 4 and, after having passed them under the bottom ring pull them with a fine crochet hook from behind to the front, so that they come out on either side of the next to last flat knot. Then pass them through above the central flat knot and bring them forward, after having passed them through from right to left and from left to right. Make a half flat knot with these threads, and let the remaining length fall in fringes in front of the work.

2nd section. Mount 153 medium green 1.50 m (1¼ yd) threads on ring 4, doubled up in the same way as those in the 1st section, but without doubling the lark's heads knots. Work diagonal double knot bars into a

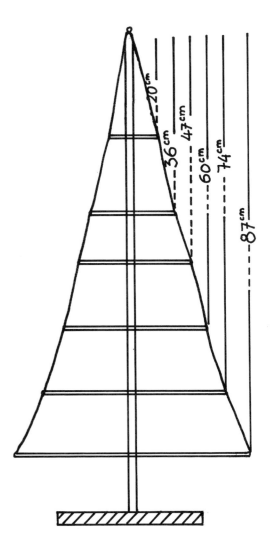

Design:
Marie-Jeanine SOLVIT

48

chevron pattern, using 8 knotting threads over one leader thread. Bring together the 6 threads lying at the bottom points of these bars of knotting, in an overhand knot; do not tie too tight. Work the intermediate threads into a knotted chain (3 knots of 3 threads over 3 threads). Work back towards the middle rows of double knots to form a diamond shape and knot the leader threads where they meet. Make a flat knot with 2 knotting threads on each side and 6 core threads. Close up in diamond-shaped bars of knotting. Knot the leader threads where they meet using an overhand knot, tied not too tightly). Leave 10 cm (4 in.) of tail on the pom-pon formed in this way. Finish the diamond shapes with an overhand knot with each thread against the bar of knotting and cut close to the knot.

3rd section. Prepare 100 medium green 1.50 m (1¼ yd) lengths and 40 dark-green 1.50 m (1¼ yd) lengths. Double-mounting as before, set on ring 3, 10 medium green threads and 4 dark green threads alternately, to give 20 medium green threads separated by 8 dark-green threads. Work a first row of diagonal double knot bars in a chevron pattern with 4 dark green threads for each leader. Use an overhand knot to bring together the dark leader threads at each point.
Next, work into a knotted chain 2 medium green threads and 4 dark-green threads. Make 10 knots and join up all the threads of 2 braids in a large overhand knot. Cut short at 2 cm (¾ in.)
On either side of this two-color motif, work a knotted chain of 7 knots with 3 threads (upper) and 2 threads (lower). With the 6 remaining medium green threads from the top, work a twisted braid of half flat knots for 13 cm (5 in.). Use an overhand knot on all the threads which made up the knotted chains on either side of the spiral braid. Make the braid stand out in the middle by joining up 2 threads from each side into a flat knot, in front of the knot made by the threads from the chain and slightly below it to keep the central twisted braid standing out. Finally, gather together all the threads hanging under these 2 knots into one large overhand knot and cut close 2 cm (¾ in.) below.

4th section. Prepare 50 medium green 1.50 m (1¼ yd) lengths and 50 light-green 1.50 m (1¼ yd) lengths. Double-mount them on ring 2, alternating 5 'medium' lengths, 5

'light' lengths, to give groups of 20 threads of each color.

Divide each group into two and make a flat knot with each half (the core thread, two knotting threads from each side).

Work a second row of alternating flat knots with the same number of threads. Take the first two lateral threads as leader and work a diagonal row of double knots up to the middle of each light green group. Then take the center threads of the central flat knot of the medium green group (3 and 3) as leader and work downwards in diagonal double knot bars parallel to the light green row of knots. Make an overhand knot with the light green leaders, then do 4 flat knots, rolled up into a flat knot ball with 4 core threads and 2 knotting threads from each side. Make 3 knots of a knotted chain 2 and 2 under this button, finishing with overhand knots, under which the thread is cut close.

Then, with the 6 light threads remaining on each side, make 4 knots of a knotted chain, finishing with 1 overhand knot over each group of 3 threads; cut close under this knot. Return to the medium green groups: between the diagonal double knot bars already worked, make 2 braids of 7 flat knots. Then take up these braids so that their base is level with the bottom of the adjacent bars of diagonal double knots, make a huge overhand knot. This keeps the braids of flat knots jutting out. Cut short the hanging threads to 1 cm (3/8 in.)

5th section. Prepare 50 light green 1.50 m (1¼ yd) lengths and 10 medium green 1.50 m (1¼ yd) lengths.

Mount them doubled on the top ring so that you have 2 medium green between 10 light green. Take on light group plus 2 medium green threads from each side. For the moment, leave the medium green threads free. Starting from the light green edge on the left, work a bar of diagonal double knot bars, covered by 3 double threads on 2 leader threads, then another, using as leader the first 2 threads to hand, on which all the threads are worked up to the center of the motif (this makes 4 knots of double threads). Work the two threads hanging under the upper knot with the 2 medium green adjacent threads, forming 10 knots of a knotted chain. Work the two following threads into a single knotted chain of 14 knots.

The two following threads are leader for a row of knotting of 2 knots. When this part of the work has been reproduced symmetrically on the right-hand half of the motif, the row of knotting from right to left will form a crossing; below this central cross, reproduce the work done on top symmetrically.

To ensure that the 14 knots of the chain take on a slightly arched shape, do not pull them too tightly before you knot them on to the double knot. Generally speaking, never tie your knots too tightly. This might spoil the attractive way wool puffs out. With the 2 double light green threads which frame the medium green, make a half flat knot. Then with its core threads, made up of four medium green threads, work 5 flat knots, rounded into a button shape and held in place with the second half of the flat knot, started above them. Leave about 5 cm (2 in.) of tail and cut short.

With the light green threads, make staggered overhand knots, beginning with one in the middle, 2 lower down, 4 below that, then 2 more and a last one in the middle. Cut the tails, following the shape of the point of the knot.

6th and last section. This is mounted on the 2.5 cm (1 in.) diameter ring with light green threads, 19 lengths of 1.20 m (1.1/3 yd) plus 1 length of 1.50 m (1¼ yd) in lark's head knots. Work downwards in a spiral row of double knots, using as leader the 2 threads from the 1.50 m (1¼ yd) length. Directly below the starting-point, after one turn of the spiral, work the threads into a single knotted chain of 8 knots.

Because the work flares out, you have to add some threads. You thus have 26 braids of knotted chain before doing the second turn of the spiral, on which you will have to add 22 more threads, spread out equally, so that you can do 12 groups of knotted chain of 4 and 4 threads.

Make 4 knots over 8 groups, twice 3 knots and twice one knot, for our spiral will now have levelled gently out into a horizontal line to finish level with the upper edge of the top ring. When you have made an overhand knot over each double thread on this last row of knotting, finish this 6th section with a bead. Now you can finish the top and the base. Some light green threads at the top, about 15 cm (6 in.) long, conceal the top of the nail under a large overhand knot and disappear into the middle of the top ring. At the bottom, between each of the medium green pom-pons in the 2nd section, add a dark green pom-pon, made up of 10 lengths of 50 cm (20 in.). There will be 17 of them.

Deck chair

You are now familiar
with flat knots and diagonal double knot bars of cording
and should have no difficulty in making this deck chair.
It will look very elegant
in any garden or on any patio.

Materials

1 deck chair frame (painted in black laquer here).
275 m (303 yd) of macramé cotton.

Method

Mount 36 lengths, each 7.60 m (8½ yd) in double lark's head knots on the top wooden bar of the deck chair. This will give you 72 threads.

The 12th thread is leader of a row of diagonal double knot bars from right to left on which the first 11 will be knotted. The 13th thread is leader of the diagonal row of double knots from left to right. The following leaders will be the threads 36 and 37, 60 and 61.

When you have picked these threads out, work alternating flat knots to fill the areas defined by these chevron-patterned bars of knots. Then, as the illustration shows, diagonal rows of double knot bars follow parallel to the first, followed by braids of 4 flat knots, framed by the same rows of knots.

Alternate with a motif of rows of knots, not parallel, but which form a diamond shape, with a center of alternating flat knots. Continue with this regular pattern, until you reach the lower row, where you finish the threads in half hitches. Strengthen with glue before cutting the threads.

Design:
Maryse DUBOULOIS

Dragonfly key-holder

This is rather like a totem pole or charm
to safeguard your house against the loss of its keys.

Materials

An old wooden spoon about 35 cm (14 in.)
long with a straight handle. Perhaps you can
find an old spoon. Otherwise use an ordinary
wooden spoon, or simply a rod.
38 m (42 yd) of rust colored wool.
12 m (13¼ yd) of sisal dyed gold.
12 m (13¼ yd) of sisal dyed royal blue.
22.80 m (25 yd) of orange wool.
30.80 m (34 yd) of dark green wool.
4 curtain hooks for broad curtain tape.
5 green ceramic beads.

Method

Mount threads on the spoon in this order:
5 rust threads of 3.80 m (4 yd).
3 gold threads of 1.50 m (1¾ yd).
4 royal blue threads of 1.50 m (1¾ yd).
3 orange threads of 3.80 m (4 yd).
8 dark green threads of 3.80 m (4 yd).
3 orange threads of 3.80 m (4 yd).
4 royal blue threads of 1.50 m (1¾ yd).
4 gold threads of 1.50 m (1¾ yd).
5 rust threads of 3.80 m (4 yd).

1st section: The 2 dark-green center threads
start off as leaders of rows of double knot
bars sloping very gently down towards the
outside. Knot 5 dark green threads over
each one. Leave the other 2 of these threads
hanging free.
Next knot 5 orange threads; use the 6th
orange thread as leader of a new horizontal
row of double knots over which 7 royal blue
threads are knotted (the first hangs free
behind), then 4 gold threads. Make the four
remaining gold threads into a flat knot. The
orange leader then makes a flat knot with 2
rust core threads and one rust thread as the
knotting thread on the left. Below, the left-
hand thread of the gold flat knot becomes
leader of a horizontal row of double knots
over which all except the last of the rust
threads are knotted. The gold leader of this
row of cording makes 2 vertical half-hitches
over this last rust thread. Then it returns as
leader of a horizontal row of double knots
left to right over which 9 rust threads are
knotted. You now have 2 gold threads behind
2 rust threads hanging free which are to be
made up into 44 vertical alternate half
hitches over these 2 gold threads.

Design: Marie-Jeanine SOLVIT

Then the orange thread makes 2 half-hitches on the pale green leader, which continues as a horizontal row of knotting over which you knot 5 pale green and 7 royal blue threads. The 8th blue thread then joins up with the pale green leader. They become core threads over which 1 dark green and 1 orange thread work alternately 15 vertical half-hitches. Reproduce symmetrically on the right part of the work.

2nd section. Continue the bars of double knot bars at the dark green center, using as leaders the free threads in the middle; this, together with the first already worked, makes 5 bars of knotting, of which the last has only one knotting thread. Cross over the leaders in the middle to join up the two parts of the work. The 4 orange threads at the side muster to outline this central motif, and the dark green leaders work over them in half-hitches after the 2 dark-green threads, left free since the work was mounted. You now have a dark-green shield shape, beneath which all the orange threads join in a large overhand knot. The last dark-green knotting thread stays free beside the central orange knot; all the rest, passing behind the two-color braids of vertical half-hitches, are worked in vertical half-hitches, over the 1st royal blue thread, pass behind the 2nd, work on the 3rd, pass behind the 4th, and so on, up to the 7th. Then make a single knotted chain braid of 5 knots with the 2 light green threads nearest to the middle, and of 4 knots with the 2 following. Continue on the right in accordance with these instructions for work on the left.

3rd section. Return to the center, taking as leader 1 orange thread under the central knot; this leads a row of knotting underlining the knots of the preceding section and turns after the 5th gold knot. Thread a green bead onto the orange leader and bring the bar of knotting back to the center where this leader is tied into a flat knot with the orange leader from opposite side over the central orange core threads. Another orange thread from the center then starts off in a row of knotting towards the outer edge and turns after the knot of the last royal blue thread. Thread a bead through it at this turning-point and continue the row back to the center. Reproduce on the right. Make another flat knot with orange leaders over the central core threads.

4th section. Return and take up the dark-green threads left on one side at the end of the 2nd section. Pass each of these behind the work to make 2 vertical half-hitches on the 5 gold threads. This gives 6 vertical rows of dark green half-hitches hiding their gold leaders.

5th section. Make an overhand knot with the 2 rust threads which have made 44 vertical half-hitches over 2 gold threads and, returning to the center, knot them in vertical half-hitches over the 7 royal blue threads; then pass behind the dark-green and royal blue thread and once more make these half-hitches on the gold and orange. Over the 2 dark green threads framing the 8 central orange threads, first make 3 flat knots, then 13 half flat knots forming a twisted braid. Repeat symmetrically on the right.

6th section. The dark-green threads return towards the center in vertical half-hitches and each forms an outside loop before joining with the flat green part; to do this,

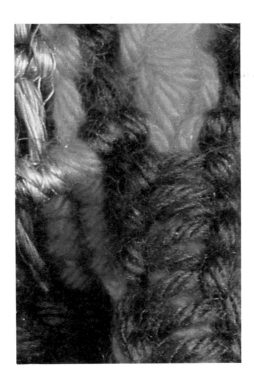

turn the piece over so that you are working on the wrong side.
Begin with the 1st dark green thread at the bottom and keep 2 of them free. Vertical half hitch over all threads at the bottom of the work. You need 16 threads in all for 4 rows on the wrong side of the work. Repeat the work on the right.
Resume work on the right side.

7th section. Return to the 8 rust threads and to the orange thread left to one side at the outer edge. Take the 1st thread on the right as leader and make 5 horizontal rows of double knots right to left. Then the leader of the 5th bar of knots returns in a V towards the center and the same work is carried out in the opposite direction for 8 bars of knotting. Then the leader threads of the 9th, 10th and 11th bar of knots are worked in vertical half-hitches over the threads which hang at the bottom of the work, up to the last royal blue thread. Now, with the two dark green threads left free at the end of the 6th section, make 6 flat knots over the two remaining

royal blue threads. Then the orange leader thread of the 14th row of knots makes vertical half-hitches over the 3rd vertical royal blue thread. 2 central orange threads pass behind the piece and return to make 5 flat knots and a half flat knot over the 2 free royal blue threads tightly holding the base prong of a curtain hook in their knot. The following rust thread makes vertical half-hitches over the 8th thread. The 2 rust threads of the central knot (those holding proud the central green spiral braid) pass behind the work to return and make 6 flat knots and a half flat knot over the 2 royal blue vertical threads to the left of the braid of orange flat knots. Now make 5 flat knots over the two vertical threads which are lying ready.
The last-but-one rust thread makes vertical half-hitches over the 6th gold thread, and waits until the last rust thread has made half-hitches over the 4th light green thread so that together with it, it makes a braid of 5 flat knots over the 5th and 6th gold threads. Take 90 cm (36 in.) of dark green thread which you cut from the center thread of the first braid of rust flat knots near the center. Use a fine crochet hook to darn in the knotting threads behind the work, and cut short the core threads of the braids of flat knots which you later strengthen at each end with transparent glue. With a very short length of dark green wool, attach the 5th bead onto the large central orange knot which is the dragonfly's head. The tail is held in a curved position by a rust knot. Under the knot, bind together rightly all the threads left at the middle with a length of rust thread. Cut close the orange threads tied up by the rust thread and make overhand knots, repeated twice, on each dark-green thread, then cut close under each knot. You now have a bunch of green balls.
For a more finished look, apply a coat of paint (using, for example, the paint sold in tiny cans for children's models) to the parts of the curtain hooks which stick out and are earmarked for hanging up the keys; otherwise use 2 coats of red nail varnish. This piece can also be used to hang tea-towels in the kitchen.
Use a fine crochet hook to darn the first green length, folded in two, on either side of the last vertical half-hitches above gold threads 3 and 4. Make a braid of 5 flat knots enclosing the prong of the second curtain hook in its knot. Do the same with the second length of dark green, but without adding the curtain hook. Repeat symmetrically on the right.

Ornamental hanging with wooden rings

Simple and easy to make.

Design: Maryse DUBOULOIS

Materials

1 medium size basket
1 small basket
3 wooden rings
40 m (44 yd) of white macramé cotton.

Method

Make a hanging loop, 10 cm (4 in.) long
overall: 3 cm (1 in.) of stem with a 7 cm
(3 in.) oval ring above it (see the instructions
for the hanging loop given on page 36.)
6 threads emerge from the base. Work these
into 3 braids of 2 threads of double-knotted
chain 46 cm (18½ in.) long.
Split each chain into two to make 2 braids
of double-knotted chain with 2 lengths only
Make these 13 cm (5¼ in.) long. You now
have 6 braids. Attach them 2 by 2 (but
separating them so that you do not take 2
braids from the same source) onto a wooden
curtain ring. Each of the two fixing threads
is knotted onto the wood with 2 half-hitches.
Four threads hang from each ring. Leave
10 cm (4 in.) free, then gather the 12
threads together in 2 rows of alternating flat
knots; and make the pom-pon. On the
opposite side of the wooden circle, start
again with twice 2 lengths on each ring which
will be made up into a double knotted chain
(with 4 threads) 30 cm (12 in.) long, then
split them up into 2 to make single knotted
chains each 10 cm (4 in.) long, then join
them again with a flat knot. Then, 9 cm
(3½ in.) of threads hang free (4 threads).
You now have 24 threads in all, which will
be joined together with two rows of staggered
flat knots. Bind them round tightly at the
bottom, then uncoil them to form the skirt
of the final 15 cm (6 in.) long pom-pon.

55

Couple on a matchbox

*After offering you a light, this couple look as though
they are ready to dance the minuet.*

Materials

2 long matchboxes
A ball of thin string
A piece of cardboard or thin wood,
9 x 12 cm (3½ x 4¾ in.)
About 12 x 15 cm (4¾ x 6 in.) light brown
fabric or suede
4 oval wooden beads
4 tiny bright blue glass beads and 24 bright
green ones.

Method

The Duke
Prepare 14 lengths, each 0.95 m (1 yd) long,
of the thinnest twine or string you can buy
in balls.
Mount the lengths in reverse lark's head knots
on the wooden part of a matchstick.
With the first 2 and last 2 threads, make a flat
knot, then the first part of a second flat knot.
Separate the knotting threads from these flat
knots, plus the next 2 threads on each side.
These 4 threads are used for the arms.
Taking as leader the next thread on the left
and on the right of the group of center
threads, work a vertical row of double knots
with the 4 threads one after the other.
Then make flat knots (1 knotting thread on
each side, 8 core threads) threading a small
royal blue glass bead, between each half of the
flat knot, onto the core thread nearest the
center of the work.
Insert all 4 beads in the same way. Next, with
the last knotting thread of the vertical rows
of double knots, keep the 4 threads which

come out of them in place. For the waist,
squeeze all the threads into a flat knot. Next,
for the flounce of the jacket, work 4 groups
of 4 flat knots (4 threads lie unused in the
middle. With a fine crochet hook, darn in
the threads hanging beneath the last flat
knots by passing them, round the back,
through the threads of the flat knot of the
waist. Separate the threads into two groups
of 10. Hold together 9 threads on each side
which are held together for the legs by the 10th
which wraps half-hitches round them. Then
work all the threads in the order in which
they come into a row of horizontal double
knots, using a match as a leader. Secure with
transparent glue.
Make 9 knots of a chain with the double
threads reserved for the arms, making the last
one looser than the rest for the cuff. Finish
the 2 threads of the cuff with an overhand
knot, and thread a wooden oval bead through
the other 2 for the hands. Do an overhand
knot and cut close.

The Duchess
Prepare 14 lengths, each 95 cm (1 yd) of the
same string.
Mount the lengths on a matchstick as for
the duke and start off the work in the same
way with a flat knot and a half flat knot.
This time, keep back 6 threads from each
side for the arms.
Then, taking as leader the first thread to the
left and to the right, work two diagonal bars
of double knot bars, curving them round
towards the middle. Next, fold up all the
thread used to make the last double knot,

Design: Marie-Jeanine SOLVIT

on the wrong side of the work, and hold them in this position with an overhand knot made with the two leaders of the last curved bar of knotting crossed over in front. For the skirt, make a flat knot in the center with 2 knotting threads and 6 core threads, to keep the fulness. Then make one flat knot on each side with the 4 remaining threads. Then make alternating flat knots, using all the threads, rounding off the hips with the threads round the edge. There are 8 rows of alternating flat knots.

Next, thread a green glass bead onto each thread before finishing off the base of the duchess with a horizontal bar of double knot bars on a long matchstick. Secure with transparent glue.

With the 6 threads reserved for the arms, make 5 staggered flat knots to give fulness to the bouffant sleeves. Thread a small glass bead on each thread; finish off with an overhand knot. Cut all the threads except the two nearest the body. With them make a single knotted chain of 3 knots and finish

the hands as shown for the duke. Glue a thin piece of wood or cardboard, covered with light brown cloth or suede on to two matchboxes placed side by side. Glue a tab under each box.

When you have cut the ends of the matchsticks sticking out beyond the mounted threads and the base of the characters, cut short the threads hanging below the bottom matchstick and glue the figures on to the brown base (which will be about 9 x 12 cm (3½ x 4 ¾ in.)).

Photo frame

Size: 46 x 32 cm (18½ x 12¾ in.)

Design:
Odile TRENTESAUX

This frame is covered with sisal dyed in different shades of red. The braids of flat knots allow you to make different size sections which can be adapted to suit the format of photos which are difficult to arrange side by side.

The frame here has been worked out to bring together 7 quite different family scenes. The threads are mounted on a leader the length of the inside perimeter of the frame. All the threads are pink, but they come in a variety of light and deep shades.

Mount 24 lengths on each of the long sides, and 16 on each short side. In all: 80 lengths, each 50 cm (20 in.)

Work the sisal in half-hitches over two leaders, forming a double bar of knotting round the opening in the center. Then leave 2 cm (¾ in.) of thread free while you outline the outside edge of the frame. As each length of knotting thread is laid alongside the leader of this last bar of knotting, you get a thicker border than the preceding horizontal double knot bars. With 12 m (13¼ yd) of violet pink string, make half-hitches right round the frame on the 2 cm (¾ in.) of thread left free between the horizontal double knot bars. These half-hitches will be worked perpendicularly to those of the rows round the frame. The braids of flat knots, which vary in width, are nailed onto the frame beneath the work around it and held in place where they cross over each other with invisible stitching.

The photograph of the finished frame shows, from left to right and from top to bottom:
1 bright pink braid of horizontal flat knots, 16 cm (6 in.) long (2 cm (¾ in.) wide).
1 pinky-red vertical braid 10 cm (4 in.) long (2 cm (¾ in.) wide).
1 paler pink vertical braid 14 cm (5½ in.) long (1.5 cm (½ in.) wide).
1 very bright pink vertical braid 9 cm (3½ in.) long (2.5 cm (1 in.) wide).
1 horizontal tea-rose pink braid 20 cm (8 in.) long (1.5 cm (½ in.) wide).
1 mauve-pink vertical braid 22 cm (8¾ in.) long (1 cm (3/8 in.) wide).

The wood of the frame is painted red to emphasize the whole color scheme.

Hedgehog

*This charming little animal,
with a pointed snout and shaggy body,
will not roll up into a ball
when a child picks it up.
Length: 16 cm (6 in.) long*

Materials

You need simple white sisal string, 5 mm (¼ in.) in diameter, and two beads (or artificial animal's eyes).

For the leaders, 3 m (3.1/3 yd) of string.
For the working threads: 50 lengths of 1.30 m (1½ yd)
Add to your estimates about 100 lengths of 15 cm (6 in.) for the prickles.

Diagram showing the course followed by the red leader thread. Add the blue threads between the red ones.

Method

Make a shape out of newspaper, on to which you pin the work (as for the bird's nest and the whale). Do it as if you were attaching two halves of a heart on to a solid shape. The leader, which starts from a point on the side near the eye, turns back on itself 5.5 cm (2 in.) from the beginning. Mount your lengths, leaving a 1 m (1 yd) length for each thread towards the top and 30 cm (12 in.) length towards the bottom. From this first turning, you do four bars of knotting before reaching the middle bottom and as you knot your half-hitches on the rows of knots lying above the starting point, slip 15 cm (6 in.) lengths of string, folded in two, under the knotting thread, allowing about 6 cm (2½ in.) to stick out for the prickles of the hedgehog. The two sides are worked in the same way, turning round the lateral row of knotting at the start. This means that the points where

Design: Odile TRENTESAUX

Belt in shades of green

You can make this very simple project in shades of several different colors to match your clothes.

Materials

20 m (22 yd) of pale green cotton
8 m (9 yd) of medium green
8 m (9 yd) of dark green

Method

Work a single knotted chain of 42 knots with 2 pale green threads 4.50 m (5 yd) long. Then, pin the knots onto the knotting board, separating the ends so that you can make 2 diagonal double knot bars with them, on which you work in double knots (half-hitches): use 1 medium green thread, 1 dark green, 1 light and 1 medium, leaving a length of 30 cm (12 in.) free on each before the 1st half-hitch.
In this way, work 4 double knot bars alongside each other. The threads form a design in which the lines forming the points run in the opposite direction to the lines of the double knot bars.
Next work the threads into a single knotted chain, letting the central braid fall straight and winding the 2 braids from either side around each other.

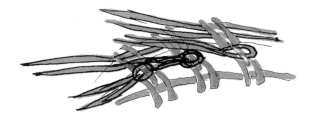

Mount threads like this to make prickles for the hedgehog.

the rows of knotting finish lie above the point of the nose. Then shape the work to a point, by slanting off the leaders, and separating the rows of knotting a little where the back bulges the most, so that you can add prickles mounted in half-hitches over the threads which pass from one row of knotting to the other.
You really should mount about 200 prickles. This is the number on the hedgehog in the photograph. He comes to life as soon as you fix his eyes, using a long needle which goes right through his head.

60

Design: Maryse DUBOULOIS

After working the central braid for 8 cm (3 in.), do 3 more diagonal double knot bars alongside each other, the leader of the 3rd coming back to the middle. In the same way, work 3 double knot bars symmetrical to the 1st 3. Then, working with the threads as they come up, do a single knotted chain of 9 knots in the middle, 12 at each side of it, then 14 down each edge. Then, 5 bars of diagonal double knots alongside each other follow in 2 groups of 4 knotting threads, separated from each other by a slit in the middle. Make a trellis pattern (see the *Glossary*) with the threads. This trellis is the middle of the belt.

Make the second half of the belt symmetrical with the first. Complete either side of the pale green central chain with knotted chains of 10 knots which you finish off with an overhand knot at the end of each thread, strengthened with a dab of transparent glue. At the other end of the belt, make similar chains to these with the lengths set aside at the start of the work. Finish them off in the same way.

Lampshade with wooden eyes

*The association of light and sight gave rise to the
idea of decorating it with eyes,
the outline shapes of which are oval bars of knotting around wooden beads.*

Materials

1 plain white cylindrical lampshade 35 cm
(14 in.) high, 32 cm (12¾ in.) in diameter.
10 brown 5 cm (2 in.) oblong wooden beads
and 5 similar beads in a light natural wood.
76 lengths of 2 m (2¼ yd) long plus 1.30 m
(1¼ yd) for the leader at the top, plus 3.45 m
(3¾ yd) for finishing off the top, plus 1.10 m
(1¼ yd) for finishing off the bottom, i.e. in
total: about 158 m (178 yd) of jute 4 mm
(1/8 in.) in diam.

Method

Take the 1.30 m (1¼ yd) length as leader
and keep it stretched horizontally while you
mount on it 76 2 m (2¼ yd) lengths in reverse
lark's head knots. The 1st thread of the 9th
length marks the center of the vertical oval
motif. Make an overhand knot 4 cm (1½ in.)
from the mounting, add a dark bead, make
an overhand knot, add a light bead, make an
overhand knot.

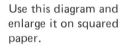

Use this diagram and
enlarge it on squared
paper.

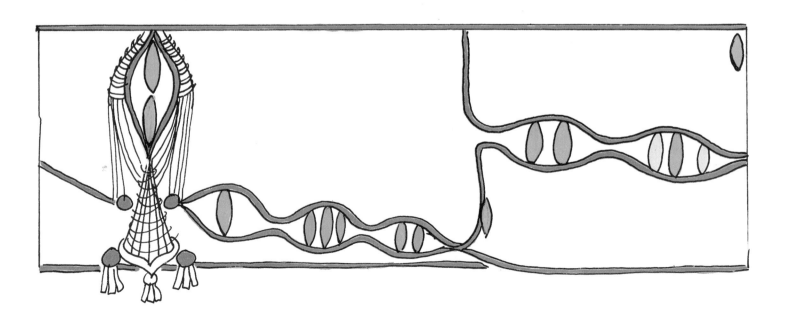

Knot the leader round the top of the lampshade. Beneath the overhand knot which keeps the circle closed, add a dark brown bead, held in place with an overhand knot over a single thread, ensures that the circle is properly finished.

Slip your diagram, enlarged on squared paper, between the lampshade and the threads.

You have one thread on either side of this center. Make a vertical half-hitch over it with the next thread. Then, with the following thread, make a half-hitch incorporating the first two, and continue in this way till you come to the 11th incorporating 10 threads. Close up the oval, first with an overhand knot, taking up together the central thread (under the light bead) and the two lateral threads. Use these 3 threads as the core of a flat knot, followed by a larger flat knot, incorporating 5 threads; make 5 flat knots in all, the last having 11 core threads.

On either side, make a first bar of diagonal double knot bars, on which you work 2 threads, then a second, joining up the middle to form the shape of the lower part of a shield. Finish with an overhand knot with 3 middle threads.

Starting with the 17th thread which marked the middle of this motif, count 83 threads; the 84th, 16 cm (6 in.) below the mounting, is turned at right angles to become the leader of an undulating bar of knotting, outlining the top contour of eye 1, then that of eye 2. It then turns and comes back from right to left, delineating their lower contours. In eye 1, place two dark brown beads, separated by 3 threads, and place 3 beads in eye 2, 3 beads: one light, one brown, one light, separated from each other by 2 threads. The leader of this bar of knotting, which finished its knots at point B, comes down vertically, and the last 2 threads which are knotted over it at the end of the bar accompany it in alternating vertical half-hitches. It finishes its course in half-hitches on the bar of knotting outlining the base of the lampshade, and it is the thread which made the left-hand half-hitches over it which will become the leader outlining eyes 3, 4 and 5, while the thread which made the right-hand half-hitches over it, will finish its course 18 cm (7 in.) below point B with an overhand knot, after it has been threaded through a brown bead which hangs vertically.

Design:
Marie-Jeanine SOLVIT

Place 2 beads, one of each color, in eye 3, then 2 brown and 1 white in eye 4, finally a single brown one in eye 5. At point C, it is one of the threads which surrounded the vertical oval at the beginning which you use as leader of the bar of knotting outlining the lower contour of eyes 5, 4, 3 and which goes on to delineate the bottom of the work up to point D, at which point you attach the leader by an overhand knot to one of the knotting threads lying to the left of 'the shield'.

To the right of the vertical oval made at the beginning at E, the two threads which follow the last thread which made the 11th half-hitch, each make a half-hitch over the next thread. Then knot the threads together in an overhand knot, and separate them again to make half-hitches over the same next thread.

Knot them together again, a few centimetres (about 1 in.) above C, and go on to join up in a large overhand knot with the holding cord of the bar of cording knotting B to C; the 3 threads of this last knot pass together behind the large flat knots lying level with point C. The threads emerging from this knot join up with the threads coming out of the knots on the top of the 'shield' bar of knotting. At point D, make a very big overhand knot with these combined threads (5 in all).

Symmetrically, on the right of the shield, make up the 5 threads hanging from the top of the work and passing behind C, in the same way into one large overhand knot.

All that remains to do now is to turn back on itself the roll made by the leader thread from the top of the lampshade and the mounting of the threads. This increases the amount that overhangs at the edge. Use a little transparent glue to stop it from from unwinding.

Tightly roll the 3.45 m (3¾ yd) length, prepared at the beginning of this work, round three times and attach it with glue on to the edge round the top of the lampshade. The 1.10 m (1¼ yd) length will be stuck on the edge round the bottom of the lampshade. Cut the fringes so that they fall a few centimetres (about 1 in.) below the rigid base of the lampshade. Use glue to help hold the wood grain effect of some of the threads that you worked without stretching between the point where you attached them on the holding cord and the bar of knotting outlining the top of the eyes.

This lampshade was made for a very old rustic, country cottage, but it also suits modern furniture and décor.

Bird's nest

Here is something to welcome winged visitors to your garden.
You can use it to house a bird you've made yourself,
like the one shown here made from resin.
You can always put a woollen bird inside it instead.

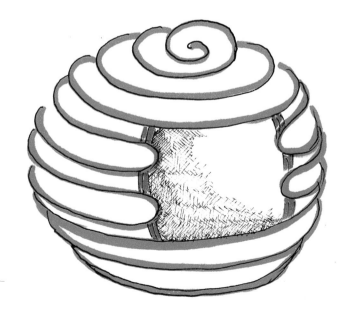

Design:
Odile TRENTESAUX

Materials

2.50 m (2¾ yd) thick sisal of 0.5 cm (¼ in.)
diameter for the leader.
About 40 lengths of baling twine, each 1.30 m
(1½ yd) long.
Newspaper.

Method

Make the round shape of the nest by making
up several small, well-shaped balls of very
damp newspaper and enclosing them in a
sheet of the same paper. This means that
when the work is finished, you will find it
easy to take the little balls out of the opening
to the nest. With a single big ball, this would
be impossible.
Starting from the middle at the top, work
a spiral bar of double knots, following the
contours of the paper ball, on to which you

pin your work as you go along. When you
get down to the level of the opening to the
nest, the leader finishes its course where the
edge of the hole is, and sets off towards the
back again, coming and going 4 times in this
way so that it works round the entrance
to the nest (see diagram). It then resumes
its spiralling path and ends up when the
work is complete at the central point at the
bottom of the nest.
Bring the threads left over at the end through
to the inside. Make a loop of twine and attach
it, as shown in the photograph, to hang up the
nest.

Two-tray hanging

An attractive and informal shelving unit
for a bedroom or
summer home.

Materials

2 square trays (the ones shown in the photograph are made from criss-crossed woven rush, attached to a frame.)

2 large wooden knitting needles, 45 cm (18 in.) long.
Jute threads: 38 lengths of 8 m (9 yd) plus 4 lengths of 3 m (3.1/3 yd) (for hanging from the ceiling) plus 6 lengths of 2.50 m (2¾ yd) and 4 lengths of 10 m (11 yd) (for the hook to hang it by) plus 1 length of 2 m (2¼ yd).
2 large wooden beads.

Method

Mount 19 lengths, each 8 m (9 yd) in double reversed half-hitches on a wooden knitting needle.

Motif 1. You have 38 threads. First make a single knotted chain of 8 knots with the 2 central threads (19 and 20). Level with the 8th central knot, work down on both sides with flat knots, using as core threads: 16-17, 13-14, 10-11, 7-8 and 4-5 and those symmetrical to them. Make 6 buttons (see the glossary) in the center with threads 19 and 20 as core threads and 18 and 21 as knotting threads.
With threads 16-17 and 22-23, make 6 overhand knots, spaced 1 cm (¼ in.) apart. Continue on either side of these 3 central braids in alternating half-hitches on a single center thread to form braids of decreasing length: 22 half-hitches, then 20, then 18, then 16, finally 11.
Edge this motif at the bottom with flat knots,

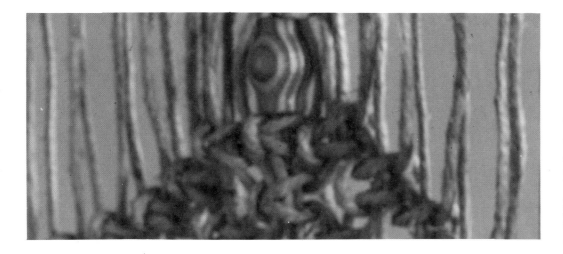

worked symmetrically to those above and finish with a single knotted chain of 8 knots. Wind the threads round one side of the frame of the first tray, passing one thread in front and one thread behind, each of which will do a double half-hitch over this frame and will join up underneath with an overhand knot.

Motif 2. Do a row of flat knots with 2 core threads and 2 knotting threads, except for the middle 1 which has 4 core threads and 2 knotting threads. Continue with alternating flat knots, decreasing on each side, so that on the 9th row you have a single flat knot in the middle.

Thread the 2 core threads through a large bead, make a flat knot under the bead and begin another 8 rows of alternating flat knots, ending up with 9 flat knots on the last row. Join the threads up in 2's with an overhand knot before attaching them to the frame of the 2nd tray in the same way that you attached the 1st. Note: attach threads 1, 2, 37 and 38 at the ends of the frame of the 2nd tray; add a length on either side, mounting them in the same way around the frame, and make them the same length as the threads next to them. This gives you 42 threads, tied in 2's with an overhand knot, ready to start on the 3rd motif.

Motif 3. With threads 1, 2, 3, 4 and 39, 40, 41, 42, make 8 flat knots. With threads 15, 16 and 27, 28, make 2 braids of 14 alternating half-hitches (single knotted chain). 3 groups of 10 threads remain; make them into 3 'windmills' as follows.

Making a 'windmill' with 10 threads:
On leader thread 1, work a diagonal double knot bar left to right with 2 and 3 as knotting threads.
On leader thread 10, work a diagonal double knot bar of right to left with 8 and 9 as knotting threads.
* On leader thread 2, work a diagonal double knot bar right to left to right with the 4 following threads as knotting threads. Leave the 2 threads on the left, and, on the 3rd thread, do a diagonal double knot bar left to right with the 2 following threads as knotting threads.
Reproduce symmetrically from right to left from * except that in the middle of the figure, on the 3rd diagonal double knot bar right to left, you work 5 half hitches instead of 2. This means that the last half hitches count as the 1st group of adjoining bars of knotting down below.

Start off again on a diagonal double knot bar left to right, with the middle thread as leader and the 2 following threads as knotting threads. Finish with a diagonal double knot bar right to left with the 5th thread as leader, over which you knot the 4 threads left on the left. Work the last diagonal double knot bar symmetrically left to right.

At the end of the flat knots on the left-hand side of this 3rd motif, use the last left-hand leader on the windmill on the left to make a flat knot incorporating 3 core threads. Do the same symmetrically on the right-hand side of this 3rd motif.

The leaders of the central windmill form a flat knot over the middle threads 15-16 and 27-28 with the leaders of the last diagonal double knot bars of the windmills at the sides. Under the middle windmill, make a large flat knot with 8 core threads and 2 knotting threads, and then go on to make a 2nd flat knot under the 1st with 15-16 and 27-28 as core threads.

Likewise, make a 2nd flat knot at either end of the motif, again with 3 core threads and 2 knotting threads. Now, under each windmill make 2 simple diagonal double knot bars, followed by a flat knot with 4 core threads. In the top part, make a single overhand knot, followed by 2 flat knots with 4 core threads. You now have groups of 3 threads which you work into 34 alternating half hitches to form the last braids of the 3rd motif of this work.

Loop to hang it by. Following the instructions for a hanging loop on page 36, make an 11 cm (4¼ in.) loop (2 cm (¾ in.) base, 9 cm (3½ in.) loop) with 6 lengths each 2.50 m (2¾ yd). Then separate the 12 threads into 4 groups of 3. Take 3 core threads for each braid, over which you work 1 length of 10 m (11 yd) will work in half flat knots for 78 cm (31 in.)

Weave in the middle thread of the 3 core threads with a fine crochet hook. After you wind the 4 threads twice round one end of the needle bearer (two threads on either side) join them together in an overhand knot. Finally, work a single knotted chain of 10 knots in 2 braids, finished off by 2 overhand knots.

Repeat this method of mounting at each end of the wooden needles.

Design:
Marie-Jeanine SOLVIT

Whale sweet and candy box

*This fun container looks best with
chocolate fishes, but you can put any types of
sweets or candy in it. It is 28 cm (11 in.) long.*

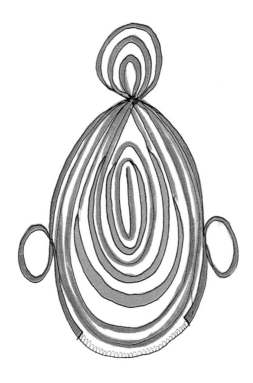

Insert the leader threads
(shown in blue) as
shown here.

Materials

Polyester string of 2 mm (1/16 in.) diameter
for the leader threads.
Polyester string of 5 mm (¼ in.) diameter.
You need about 20 m (22 yd) of 5 mm (¼ in.)
string for the labyrinth of leaders. Prepare
1.40 m (1½ yd) lengths of polyester string;
the number will vary according to the size of
the part of your egg-shaped work. There are
80 in the widest section round the edges of
the opening.

Method

Prepare a damp newspaper mould (shape)
filled with little balls. Your mould (shape)
should be a 20 cm (8 in.) long oval, rounded
at one end and pointed at the other. The
circumference of the rounded end (the
whale's head) ought to measure about 30 cm
(12 in.) (Refer to bird's nest project on page
65 for more details on how to make the
mould (shape)).
Begin at the top of the diagram 5 cm (2 in.)
below the point, by laying out with the 5 mm
(¼ in.) diameter string, a leader thread for a
bar of double knots. The leader will turn
and run back on itself.
Mount lengths of the 2 mm (1/16 in.)

Design: Odile TRENTESAUX

diameter string on 9 cm (3½ in.) of this leader. It comes back on itself along the 9 cm (3½ in.) of the start, then turns (head end), goes back towards the tail and draws away to allow room to insert, head end, an extra length of leader thread, which fills up the round shape with its circular arc, 15 cm (6 in.) long. The 1st leader goes around this inserted length, then draws away from it to continue following the rounded part which makes the head end bigger. Insert 2 more separate leader threads every other time you go around, starting off respectively 12 cm (4¾ in.) and 13 cm (5¼ in.) from the point at the tail end.

Starting from the 1st loop formed at the beginning by the leader (head end), you have 9 bars of knots to cover with half hitches completing the bottom half of the work.

But, on the 8th row at each side about 10 cm (4 in.) from the rounded part, your leader thread forms a loop which sticks out, on which you wind a single thread around to continue the design made by the half hitches on the bar of knotting; this represents the fins (as you can see in the photograph).

At the tail end, your last 2 bars of knots form loops in the same way — for the tail, sticking out 4 cm (1½ in.) then 5 cm (2 in.) from the point at the back.

Start off again with a leader thread. Begin by forming a tail loop before going around the paper shape.

Add 19 lengths to the leader to form the edge of the upper jaw. The 2 halves of the work join up all the way around from this point. The same work, with lengths added between 2 bars of double knotting, makes up the upper half. In the middle, the threads, held in place by fine string ties around them 8 times spurt out like the water a whale expels through its blow-hole. Leave them 16 to 17 cm (about 6 in.) long.

The 2 wooden beads become the eyes of the whale. Sew them between the 2 rows of knots above the corner of the mouth.

A short tie holds the loops of the tail together at the point at the back. Your whale now only has to spit out its little balls of paper stuffing.

When this model was made, the artist made a bar of double knots to join the 2 halves of the whale by turning the bottom half of the half finished work inside out like a glove. This gives a reverse pattern to the middle row of knotting, as you can see in the photograph.

An easier way to do this is to join the 2 halves of the work by threading a string in a lattice pattern all around the edges of each piece.

Ball lampshade

The hidden surface of macramé work always differs
from that which you look at.
The unifying effect comes from
the fibres which make up the macramé. Here, they
have the genuine look of natural materials.

Materials

1 spherical lampshade frame 40 cm (16 in.) in diameter.
About 100 lengths 1.5 to 2 m (1½ to 2¼ yd) long of assorted fibres: for example, sisal, natural colored baling twine, baling twine dyed brown, baling twine dyed light brown, different thicknesses of jute, thick natural colored cotton, thick cotton dyed orange, rug wool, and so on.

Method

Hold strands of baling twine in place against the top ring of the frame, from which 8 double knot bars wind down around the sphere in a rather irregular spiral.

Use different threads to make half hitches over these bars of double knots. Put in some orange, brown and light brown lengths — 1 of each color on 2 opposite sides. You will see that, because the line the threads follow around the work is wholly on the bias (never on the vertical because that lacks imagination) their finishing point at the bottom of the sphere is a quarter of a circle further over to the left than their starting point.

Use another length of brown baling twine to separate the white away from the lighter fibres of the work, the 3 adjacent threads on the right.

The greyish tones of the fibres temper that of the orange threads besides it. Fill gaps between the oblique double knots here and there with wick wool, rug wool, jute or tow. Pass these strands alternately over and under the perpendicular threads like lattice work. Where the diameter of the sphere gets bigger, add a number of threads onto the oblique double knot bars. They disappear again when the surface you are covering narrows towards the bottom; conceal the ends of the threads behind the threads next to them, after you have fastened them in half-hitches on a descending row of knotting.

The hairier fibres hide the light-bulb. Work them into a trellis pattern (see the glossary) on the warp formed by the vertical threads.

Design: Odile TRENTESAUX

Wind several strands round the electric flex (cord) connecting the ball to the ceiling and hold them in place with invisible nylon thread.

Improvise and use your imagination when working on this project. You do not need any more exact instructions.

The result will be unique. Don't use a very high powered electric light bulb. Bright lights get very hot and can cause a fire.

Room divider with separate panels

*This piece consists of different macramé sections and
can be adapted to any width opening.*

Each part is decorated with a different design;
this makes this room divider particularly
lively and original. You can hang it equally
well from the rings of a curtain rod or on a
fixed wooden rod. Each panel measures
20 cm (8 in.) wide by 1.90 m (2 yd) high.

Materials for each section

1 wooden support 20 cm (8 in.) long.
According to the model, 15 or 16 lengths of,
on the average, 10 m (11 yd) of polyester
string 2.5 mm (1/16 in.) in diameter. (could
also be sisal or any other fibre).

Method

1st section: Mount 16 lengths, each 10 m
(11 yd) long on the 20 cm (8 in.) length of
wood. Let them fall free for 30 cm (12 in.).
Then make braids of knots for 30 cm (12 in.),
each with 4 threads:
1) twisted braid of half flat knots.
2) 2 half flat knots partly separated from the
following ones by a gap of 2 cm (¾ in.)
crossing the threads over so those which have
done the knotting become the core threads
and *vice-versa*.
3) 2 braids worked together in alternating
flat knots, 1 cm (3/8 in.) apart, with, half-
way down in the middle, a large pea (see the
glossary) of 4 flat knots.
4) 10 cm (4 in.) twisted braid of half flat
knots, a large loop with the knotting threads,

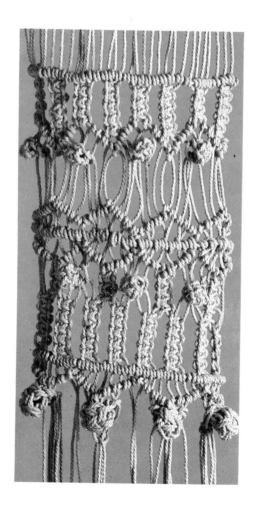

2 flat knots, a large loop and another twisted
braid of half flat knots.
5) 6 groups of 4 flat knots each separated by
an overhand knot with the core threads.
6) 2 braids worked together.
On the 8 available threads, first of all work
the 4 central threads into 2 times 2 flat knots,
the last 2 having 4 core threads, then 3 flat
knots 2.5 cm (1 in.) lower down, with 6 core
threads; 2 cm (¾ in.) lower down: 2 times 2
flat knots side by side. They mark the middle
of this motif. Reproduce the bottom half
symmetrically.
Next, let the threads fall free for 20 cm (8 in.).
A horizontal double knot bar holds all the
threads together (the leader is the 1st thread).
Then, make 8 braids of 5 flat knots, diagonal
double knot bars in a chevron pattern, with
the core threads, and between the points of
these chevrons, a large pea of 4 flat knots.
Now, 4 cm (1½ in.) from the points of the
chevrons, make diagonal double knot bars
again, facing the 1st ones. Make a horizontal
double knot bar across the whole width (with
the 1st thread as leader), the diagonal double
knot bars, symmetrical with those lying
above the horizontal bar.
Make 4 braids of 3 flat knots and a half flat
knot under each point of the diagonal bars,
between which you place a large pea of 4
flat knots. Then make 8 staggered braids
of 5 flat knots, underlined by a horizontal
double knot bar (the leader is the 1st thread
on the left).

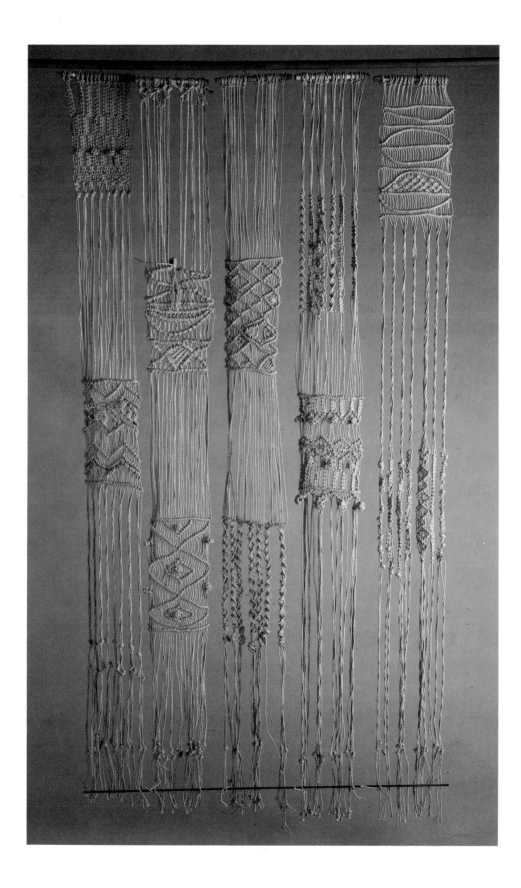

Then do 4 groups of diagonal double knot bars in a chevron pattern, each finishing with a big pea of 4 flat knots made with 3 core threads and 2 knotting threads on each side. Let the threads fall to an overhand knot joining up the threads in 2's 15 cm (6 in.) from the bottom. Finish with an overhand knot at the bottom of each thread.

2nd section: Mount 15 lengths, each 10 m (11 yd) on the 20 cm (8 in.) piece of wood. After letting the threads fall free for 45 cm (18 in.), do a horizontal double knot bar followed by bars of double knots in diamond shapes: do 6 double knot bars on the 1st row, a diamond 18 threads wide to the left of a small one of 8 threads. Under the latter, small diamonds of 8 threads bring you down level with the bottom of the large diamond (1 large knot in the middle of the 3rd small diamond on the right). Then continue the small diamonds on the left-hand side, while you form a diamond 18 threads wide with double sides on the right of the work. On the left, beneath this big diamond, decorate the middle of a small 1 with 4 alternating flat knots.
The last little diamond, on the bottom right, has a middle worked in a trellis (see the *Glossary*) pattern. A horizontal double knot bar closes this motif 28 cm (11 in.) from the horizontal double knot bar at the start.
After letting the threads fall free for 40 cm (16 in.) make a horizontal double knot bar to hold the threads in place side by side. Next work braids of half flat knots, 30 cm (12 in.) long, ending with a large overhand knot with 4 threads.
About 15 cm (6 in.) from the bottom, make overhand knots, taking the threads 2 by 2, and an overhand knot at the end of each.

3rd section: Mount 16 lengths, each 10 m (11 yd) on the 20 cm (8 in.) long piece of wood. About 6 cm (2¼ in.) from the start, using the 1st thread, do a horizontal double knot bar which you work back in a curved shape, falling 3 cm (1¼ in.) below the higher double knot bar, then climbing up again towards it and stopping 2 threads away from the left-hand side.
Take up the last thread on the right to make another horizontal double knot bar 5 cm (2 in.) lower down than the 1st.
The leader falls free for 5 cm (2 in.) on the left before climbing up again in a circular

Design:
Odile TRENTESAUX

arc to form the upper half of a regular oval shape, crossed through the middle with horizontal double knot bar. After the circular arc at the bottom of the oval, the leader comes out again on the right.

Make a horizontal double knot bar, followed by a 2nd oval, which, like the 1st is 9 cm (3½ in.) high by 20 cm (8 in.) wide, but the top half of which is worked in alternating flat knots. It is underlined by a last horizontal double knot bar. Then the threads hang free for 65 cm (26 in.).

Divide the threads into groups of 4; then knot them into 30 cm (12 in.) long braids in the same way as those in the 1st section above except for 1 group made up of 8 threads (see the photograph for the placement of this section).

This section is made into diamonds, using threads 1 and 8 as leaders, and separated by smaller ones, leaving 1 thread free on each side. Decorate the middle of the big diamonds with a trellis (see the *Glossary*), then with a large flat knot.

Finish with 2 flat knots with 6 core threads. Knot all the threads in 2's 15 cm (6 in.) from the bottom.

4th section: Mount 16 lengths, each 10 m (11 yd) on the 20 cm (8 in.) long, length of wood.

Begin with 8 braids of 8 flat knots, followed by 2 rows of braids of 5 knots. Then make 4 big peas of 4 flat knots, followed by 7 staggered braids of 4 flat knots, then 8 staggered braids of 3 flat knots, 7 of 2 flat knots and finally 8 flat knots.

Make a large overhand knot with the 4 threads of each flat knot 1 cm (¼ in.) lower down. Then let the threads fall free for 50 cm (20 in.).

Next, make a horizontal double knot bar, beneath which you make 4 bars of diagonal double knots in a chevron pattern, followed, 3 cm (1¼ in.) lower down by bars of double knots parallel to them.

Underneath the 2 high points formed in this way, make a big pea (see the *Glossary*) of 4 flat knots, then 8 7 cm (2¾ in.) long braids of half flat knots.

Once again, make 4 diagonal double knot bars parallel to the preceding ones, followed by the same pattern, again 7 cm (2¾ in.) lower down.

Make 4 double diagonal double knot bars 3 cm (1¼ in.) below and again parallel with the preceding ones. Complete this motif by an underline of a final horizontal double knot bar.

Let the threads fall free for 45 cm (18 in.).

A large overhand knot holds the threads in 4s. Then, 5 cm (2 in.) lower down, an overhand knot holds them in 2s. Repeat the same knotting 20 cm (8 in.) lower down.

5th section: Mount 15 threads, each 10 m (11 yd) long on the 20 cm (8 in.) length of wood. After letting the threads fall free for 47 cm (19 in.), place a large pea between threads 16 and 17, made with 4 inserted threads each 3.85 m (4¼ yd) long, plus 2 small knotting threads (which make the 4 flat knots of the large pea, plus the flat knot to hold it). Make a 12 cm (4¾ in.) tail below this large pea.

These threads draw aside from the large pea and become double leaders of diagonal double knot bars which slope gently down until they meet the sides again. Then they return to the middle, cross over each other, and set off towards the edges again.

Next, do 2 parallel horizontal double knot bars. Underline them by a slightly curved bar, then a 2nd semi-circular bar.

Let the 2 threads at each end of this bar fall vertically for 9 cm (3½ in.). Then they become leaders of a horizontal double knot bar. They cross in the middle, form a diamond shape (decorated in the middle with a trellis), continue to the edge and finish on the horizontal.

You have 4 more threads than at the start. Let them fall free for 40 cm (16 in.). Then use the last thread on the right as leader of a horizontal double knot bar. Threads 9 and 22 then become leaders of V-shaped diagonal double knot bars, the point of which lies below a central large pea of 4 flat knots.

With the 1st and last threads as leaders, return to the middle with diagonal double knot bars, cross over and set off towards the edges again, after 1st placing 1 large pea on each side of the work, level with the cross-over of the bars of knots.

Now make a small central diamond with 7 knotting threads on each side, decorated in its middle with a large pea. Your 2 leaders close up the large diamond.

Repeat this motif, not forgetting the large peas at the sides. Finally, underline the motif with a last horizontal double knot bar, before knotting the threads 2 by 2, 15 cm (6 in.) from the bottom, then again 2 by 2, but staggered this time, 2 cm (¾ in.) lower down. Think up another design if you want a wider room divider.

To avoid any problems arising from the threads slipping off the 20 cm (8 in.) wood lengths, secure the threads at the ends with a staple.

Red wire necklace

*This light but emphatic piece
looks superb
with a low-cut neckline.*

Design: Maryse DUBOULOIS

Materials

0.39 m (½ yd) of fine macramé cotton
A reel of fine red plastic-covered wire.

Method

Wind the wire around the length of macramé
cotton, pulling the loops tightly against each
other. Carefully make a hook at 1 end by
twisting 2 short strands of wire together.
At the other end, make a ring to fasten the
necklace.
Then mount 16 lengths of metallic thread

as follows: 4 40 cm (16 in.) long at each
end and 8 70 cm (28 in.) long in the middle.
Work a 1st section of 8 braids, each with 4
flat knots, then 7 staggered braids, then 6.
Between the 4 middle braids insert 3 spiral
braids of 15 half flat knots. Add 2 lengths
between the central threads lying to the right
and left of the central column, and work 2
new braids of the same length.
Finish by cutting off the threads under the
3 braids lying on the edges of the necklace
and those which stick out below the central
spiral braids, pinching them back so they are
rounded and do not scratch.

Portico frame

Design:
Marie-Jeanine SOLVIT

Standard — 2 knots

The frame outlines the area of the wall on which a collection of necklaces or other objects is arranged. It can also be used as a frame for a rectangular mirror, the base of which rests on a shelving unit.

Materials

A length of wooden dowelling 1.05 m (41 in.) long.
273.60 m (300 yd) of macramé cotton 3 mm (3/16 in.) in diameter.

Method

Prepare 16 lengths of 9.60 m (10½ yd) and 80 lengths of 1.50 m, (60 in.). Mount them on the dowelling thread bearer in double reverse lark's head knots like this: 8 lengths of 9.60 m (10½ yd), 80 lengths of 1.50 m (60 in.) and 8 lengths of 9.60 m (10½ yd)

1) Left-hand column: is made with the first 8 lengths of 9.60 m (10½ yd)

Section 1: With threads 1, 2, 3, 4 and 13, 14, 15, 16, make 5 alternating vertical half-hitches with double thread. Threads 5 and 12 will be leaders of double knot bars which cross over each other in the middle with a flat knot. Before making the diamond, that is decorated with a flat knot with 8 core threads, do three overhand knots with the threads which surround it. At the bottom of this diamond, tie the leader threads together with an overhand knot. On the 1st thread, 6 overhand knots, on the 2nd: 5 overhand knots, on the 3rd: 4 overhand knots, on the 4th: 4 overhand knots, on the 5th: 3 overhand knots, on the 6th and 7th: 1 overhand knot.

Section 2: Take up the 2 middle threads as leaders of a second diamond, and work the middle like this: 1 flat knot with the 4 middle threads, an X in diagonal double knot bars with an overhand knot tying the 2 leaders together in the middle of the diamond. Work a flat knot on its left, one on its right and a flat knot below, again with the 4 middle threads. Complete the diamond with an overhand knot, joining up its leaders. Then, with threads 1 and 2, make a single knotted chain of 9 knots; with threads 3 and 4, a single knotted chain of 6 knots. Do the same symmetrically on the right.

Section 3: Take up the 2 middle threads to form the following diagonal double knot bars. Make 4 alternating vertical double knots with the first 4 threads lying on the left, then a single knotted chain of 3 knots with the 2 following threads, then an overhand knot with the 2 following threads. With the 2 threads remaining in the middle, make a single knotted chain of 3 knots. Repeat this symmetrically on the right. Your middle threads will again be leaders of bars of diagonal cording forming a new diamond, inside which you will make 3 spiral braids of half-knots (separated by a non-working thread). The one in the middle will have 14 half knots; each of the other two, 6 half knots. Underneath this diamond, do knots symmetrical with those made above it, as well as diagonal double knot bars symmetrical with those at the beginning of this 3rd section.

Section 4: Do 4 overhand knots with the 2 middle threads. Then on either side work a single knotted chain of 10 knots, a plait with 3 strands, and a single knotted chain of 10 knots. Finish with 2 diagonal double knot bars lying alongside each other, bringing the leader back to the middle.

Section 5: With the first 3 and last 3 threads, make 9 alternating, vertical double knots. Cross over the middle threads to form a diamond, and work the middle in trellis pattern. At its base do an overhand knot.

Section 6: Work single knotted chains all over like this: 10, 8, 6, 3 (and repeat symmetrically on the right). With the 2 middle threads make slightly sloping diagonal double knot bars. An overhand knot in the middle, separated by 2 threads from 2 more overhand knots, then take back the leaders horizontally to the middle 2 bars of knots, and join up together again in an overhand knot.

Section 7: The middle threads set off again to form a diamond, in which the 4th and 6th threads (starting from the middle will be leaders of diagonal double knot bars, and finish off with an overhand knot. Similarly, do an overhand knot at the bottom of this diamond.

Section 8: With threads 1, 2, 3: a spiral braid of 9 half knots. Repeat with threads 4, 5, 6 (these spiral braids have only one core thread). Then, thread 7 makes 5 vertical double knots with thread 8. Repeat symmetrically on the right. Finish off this section with bars of knotting moving back to the middle in the shape of the bottom of a shield. Work an overhand knot in the middle.

Section 9: With the first 2 threads and the last 2, make a single knotted chain of 11 knots, then take the 2 middle threads as leaders of diagonal double knot bars, over which only 2 threads are knotted. Next, take the 2nd free thread from the middle, which will be leader of a diagonal double knot bar covered with 3 knotting threads. You then make a flat knot with the 4 middle threads, the following threads being leader of a third diagonal double knot bar, over which 5 threads are knotted. This brings it back to the outside edge of the figure. When you have done the same symmetrically, do 3 rows of alternating flat knots, following beside this last bar of knotting, and a flat knot in the middle (with 6 core and 2 knotting threads). This central flat knot marks the geometric center of this 9th section. Work the bottom half symmetrically to the one you have just done, and finish with a flat knot in the middle, followed by an overhand knot, marking the starting point of the leaders which move away from each other in a horizontal double knot bar.

Section 10: The 2 middle threads cross over each other and become leaders of diagonal double knot bars, over which 5 threads work. The 2 threads at either end make a single knotted chain of 5 knots. Then the 2 middle threads cross over each other and become leaders of bars of cording to describe a diamond shape, the middle of which is decorated with overhand knots. An overhand knot joins up the leaders in the middle.

Section 11: With the first 3 threads, make 12 alternating, vertical double knots. With the 2 following threads make a single knotted chain of 11 knots. With the 2 following threads make a single knotted chain of 9 knots. The 2 middle threads remain free. Repeat symmetrically on the right. With the 1st and last threads as leaders, take 2 diagonal double knot bars to the middle, where you make an overhand knot.

2) Motifs along the top: There are 10 motifs, each worked with 16 threads.

1st motif: Do 4 flat knots. An overhand knot on threads 5, 8, 9 and 12. Below, an overhand knot joining 8 and 9. The threads from either end will be leaders of diagonal double knot bars and will join up in the middle in an overhand knot. With threads 1 and 2, then 3 and 4, do a single knotted chain of 8 knots. Do 3 overhand knots on thread 5. Threads 6, 7 and 8 will make 8 alternating, vertical half hitches. Do the same symmetrically on the right. Finish off with overhand knots, keeping back in the middle these threads in twos: 2 and 3, 4 and 5, 8 and 9. Do the same symmetrically.

2nd motif: Do an overhand knot on threads 1 and 16 and an overhand knot, joining 4 to 5 and 12 to 13. An overhand knot joins the 2 middle threads which then become leaders to form a diamond, in the middle of which is a large flat knot with 8 core and 2 knotting threads. Then do an overhand knot on threads 1 and 16, all the other threads being joined up in twos with overhand knots. A last row of staggered overhand knots completes this motif. Cut the threads close.

3rd motif: Do a single knotted chain of 3 knots with threads 1 and 2 and 15 and 16. With 3, 4, 5, 6 and 11, 12, 13, 14, make: a flat knot, an overhand knot, a flat knot, an overhand knot. With the 4 central threads, make a spiral braid of 11 half flat knots. Then lead back to the middle, 3 bars of diagonal knotting lying alongside, then join up the leaders of the 3 bars of knotting in a central overhand knot. To finish off, do an overhand knot on each thread. Cut close.

4th motif: Make a flat knot in the middle. Threads 1 and 16 will be leaders of diagonal double knot bars which are brought back to the middle. After you have made an overhand knot just above and just below this bar of cording, on threads 7, 8, 9 and 10, cut them close. Do a single knotted chain of 13 knots on the first 2 threads, then 9 half knots with 3 and 5 on 4. Repeat symmetrically on the right. Do an overhand knot with the 2 middle threads which will then lead a bar of very steep diagonal knotting. The leader threads will then become knotting threads of a large central flat knot embracing 10 threads. Finish off with an overhand knot at the end

of each. Cut close.

5th motif: Do staggered overhand knots on 1, 2, 3, 4 and 13, 14, 15, 16. Then a diamond in which 2 braids of alternating vertical double knots will cross over each other. Join the middle threads with 2 successive overhand knots. Work a single knotted chain of 6 knots with 1 and 2, 15 and 16. Then a single knotted chain of 5 knots with 3 and 4, 13 and 14. And 2 flat knots with 5, 6, 7, 8 and 9, 10, 11, 12. Finish off with overhand knots and cut close.

6th motif: Do 3 centered flat knots, a diagonal double knot bar, taking leaders 1 and 16 to the middle, above which you will have made an overhand knot joining 7-8 and 9-10. After making an overhand knot on the leaders in the middle, work down a second bar of knotting, 1 cm (½ in.) below and parallel to the first. Overhand knot with the leaders in the middle and overhand knots to finish off the threads. Cut close.

7th motif: Do 4, then 3, then 2, then 1 staggered flat knots. Underline this triangle with 2 diagonal double knot bars joining them up in an overhand knot in the middle. Do a second diagonal double knot bar separated from the first by 1.5 cm (5/8 in.). Make an overhand knot in the middle with the leaders. Join in an overhand knot 1-2-3 and 14-15-16 and cut. Threads 4 and 13 will be leaders to take a bar of knotting towards the middle lying alongside the preceding one and finished off with an overhand knot. Finish off each of the other threads with an overhand knot and cut close.

8th motif: Do 2 overhand knots 2 cm (7/8 in.) away from each other, joining up the middle threads. Then make bars of knotting into a 'windmill' with: 1st leader, thread 1, over which the 4 following threads will work; 2nd leader, the 3rd thread to hand, over which 4 threads work; the 3rd leader is the 5th thread to hand, over which 3 threads work. Repeat symmetrically on the right. Using as leaders the 2 middle threads, cross them over in the middle and do two last bars of knotting. 4 threads will work over each. Then, make an overhand knot and cut close. With the remaining threads: 1, 2, 3 and 14, 15, 16, do 12 alternating vertical double knots. An overhand knot joins these 3 threads up, then cut close.

9th motif: Next you do an X in bars of diagonal knotting, crossing over at the middle. They then return to the middle and outline a small flattened diamond, decorated in the middle by a flat knot with 6 core and 2 knotting threads. Do an overhand knot to finish off each thread, a knot to join the 2 middle threads together, and cut close.

10th motif: Do an overhand knot, joining the 2 middle threads. Take as leaders of bars of diagonal knotting, the threads: 1, 8, 9 and 16; 3 threads will be knotted over each. Join up the leaders with an overhand knot and work down again symmetrically, making a trellis with the threads from the central diamond and making 6 half knots with the first 3 and last 3 threads, before knotting them over the continuation of the bars of diagonal knotting. Then make a spiral braid of 7 half knots in the middle, surrounded by braids of 4 alternating vertical double knots, then 3. Do an overhand knot at the end of threads 1, 2, 5, 6, 7 and the threads symmetrical to them. When the threads 3, 4, 8, 9 and 13, 14 have been joined in overhand knots, cut close.

3) Right-hand braid:

Section 1: Do 4 flat knots, then stagger 3, 2, 1 more. Underline with 2 bars of diagonal knotting, joining them up together with a central overhand knot, followed by a flat knot and another overhand knot, and work the lateral threads, making single knotted chains of 8, 12 and 15 knots symmetrically.

Section 2: Using 8 and 9 as leaders, make a diamond, in the middle of which 2 braids of 11 alternating vertical double knots cross over each other.

Section 3: Threads 1, 2, 3 and 14, 15, 16 make 8 alternating vertical double knots. Threads 5, 6, 7 and 10, 11, 12 make 7 of them. The 2 central threads join up in 3 overhand knots spaced 1 cm (½ in.) apart.

Section 4: Threads 1 and 16 lead 2 bars of diagonal knotting to the middle. Join up the first 2 and last 2 threads in 4 successive overhand knots. Do 6 alternating vertical double knots with 3, 4, 5 and 12, 13, 14. Cross over the leaders in the middle and set off in diagonal double knot bars towards the outside.

5th section: In the middle, make a large flat knot with 8 core and 2 knotting threads and bring back the bars of knotting to the middle to close up the diamond which is completed by a central overhand knot. 1.5 cm (5/8 in.) from this last bar of knotting, join up threads 1 and 2, 3 and 4, 5 and 6 with overhand knots. A central flat knot will be followed by a flat knot with 4 core threads. Join up 2 and 3, 4 and 5, 12 and 13, 14 and 15 with

overhand knots. Make 2 overhand knots on 1 and 16, 1.5 cm (5/8 in.) apart.

Section 6: Take 2 diagonal double knot bars towards the middle and join them with an overhand knot. Do overhand knots on all the threads except 8 and 9 which will make a single knotted chain of 3 knots. Make another 2 diagonal double knot bars and having brought them to the middle, join up their leaders with an overhand knot.

Section 7: Do a single knotted chain of 10 knots on 1 and 2, 15 and 16, then 6 alternating vertical half hitches with 3, 4, 5 and 12, 13, 14, then a single knotted chain of 3 knots, either side of the middle. Next, make a diamond. In its middle, put: 2 crossover braids made from single knotted chains of 9 knots using threads 5-6 and 11-12, and 2 overhand knots on threads 3, 4 and 13, 14. Finish with an overhand knot joining the leaders in the middle.

8th section: 1 cm (½ in.) below this diamond, do an overhand knot on 2, 4, 6 and 11, 13, 15. Then a second overhand knot 1 cm (½ in.) lower down on 2 and 15. Start off from the middle with 2 slightly sloping diagonal double knot bars, then take them back to the middle, outlining convex curves with the leaders, after having crossed over 6, 7, 8 and 9, 10, 11 in the middle. Join the leaders together in a central overhand knot. 1 and 16 will be leaders of diagonal double knot bars which cross over in the middle and go off again almost on the horizontal, to return in the same manner towards the middle. Overhand knot on the leaders in the middle.

9th section: 3 times in succession, take diagonal double knot bars down in a fan shape from the middle towards the outside, and between each of them do 2 overhand knots on 1 and 2 and 15 and 16. Beneath the last, make single knotted chains like this: 6 on 7-8 and 9-10; 4 on 5-6 and 11-12; 2 on 3-4 and 14.

Then join up in overhand knots threads 2-3, 4-5, 6-7, 8-9 and those symmetrical to them, and underline with 2 diagonal double knot bars brought back towards the middle in the shape of the bottom of a shield.

10th section: Work a downward slope of flat knots in 3 staggered rows. Make a large flat knot in the middle with 6 core and 2 knotting threads, and make another 3 staggered rows symmetrical with those above. Finish with an overhand knot, joining the 2 central threads together.

Rustic pot-holder

Here is something to hang on your kitchen wall,
always ready to protect a surface
or a work-top
from the bottom of a saucepan.

Design: Odile TRENTESAUX

Materials

42. 60 m (48 yd) of baling twine in triple
ply: 3 lengths of 1 m (1 yd) for the perimeter
3 lengths of 3.20 m (3½ yd) for the leader
thread and 12 lengths 2.50 m (2¾ yd)

Method

Hammer 4 nails into the knotting board to mark the corners of the
24 x 24 cm (9½ x 9½ in.) square. Lay out the 3 lengths of 1 m (1 yd)
together, to make up the length for the perimeter of the work.
Begin at the corner opposite the one where you put in the suspension
ring (2 lengths of the perimeter thread, around which you wind the
3rd to cover the ring).
Keep 3 lengths of 2 m (2¼ yd) on 1 side of the 1st loop made in the
work; on the other side, there will be 3 threads of 1.20 m (1.1/3 yd).
The 3 lengths of 3.20 m (3½ yd) are laid out in this way, to make,
with the 2 m (2¼ yd) threads, the whole length of the leader for the
row of double knots which cuts across the work, and, with the
1.20 m (1.1/3 yd) threads, the half hitches, form the 1st left-hand
braid, parallel to the left-hand side of the square (seen with the hanging
hook at bottom right).
The left-hand threads pass in front of those on the left side of the
perimeter and reappear behind to form the top horizontal double
knot bar, whereas those on the right pass in front of the threads at
the top of the perimeter and return from behind (half hitch) to be
knotted onto the 1st horizontal double knot bar.
Mount the 4 triple lengths which remain in reverse lark's head knots
onto the top perimeter and work them over the horizontal double
knot bars parallel to this thread bearer.

Follow the photograph to work out the route of the triple thread
which decides the shape of these bars of knots. Between the 1st and
the 2nd, work a row of half hitches in the opposite direction over
the threads which connect the 2 bars of knotting together.
Do the same between the 3rd and 4th, whereas the 1st time, you
worked a single thread, the 2nd time, use a triple thread. When the
threads arrive at the bottom of the perimeter, they make half hitches
over it, then slip up against the threads of the last horizontal double
knot bar. The end of their path is hidden by the half hitches you made
over this bar of knotting.
Each time the leader of the horizontal double knot bars reaches 1
of the side edges of the perimeter, it forms a double half hitch over
it before going on its way again.
To complete the work, tie an overhand knot tightly around the
base of the suspension ring.

Fancy wall light in white cotton

*This fixture will soften the light that it filters
as well as the room it is in.*

Materials

1 wall light frame, 25 cm (10 in.) wide,
18 cm (7 in.) high, 13 cm (5 in.) deep
1 piece of white jersey fabric 75 x 22 cm
(30 x 9 in.) for the lining (this will be put
in last)
50 m (5½ yd) of heavy white cotton thread.

Method

Mount 46 lengths, each 1 m (1 yd) long
straight onto the top of the frame (front and
sides only) in reverse lark's head knots.
Using the rest of the cotton for a leader, make
a horizontal double knot bar, 11 cm (4¼ in.)
from the mounting of the threads.
With the 7th thread preceding the middle
of the work and the 7th thread after it, make
the leaders of 2 diagonally descending
double knot bars, each of which you work
over by 6 threads. Continue the diagonal
double knot bars with 6 knotting threads
over 1 leader all around up to the bar which
marks the back of the lampshade. (At either
end, after your 6 knotting threads, you have
the leader of the horizontal double knot
bar which drops down towards the bottom
of the work where it again becomes leader
of the horizontal double knot bar at the
bottom.

Next work in 'lace' stitch. To do this, at the
top of a diamond shape, pick out 4 threads,
2 on the left and 2 on the right of the peak.
Call these 1, 2, 2, 4.
Cross 1 over 2 and 3 over 4 (diagram 1). Then
work your threads as for trellis stitch (see
the *Glossary*) in such a way that the thread
on top passes next beneath the following
one, and *vice-versa*.

Diagram 2

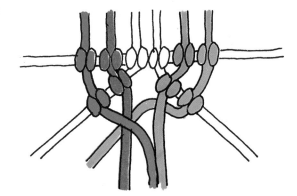

Diagram 1

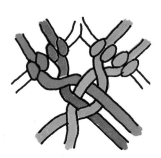

Diagram 3

Design: Odile TRENTESAUX

Thread 1 then passes in turn over 2, under 4 and over 3.

Thread 2 passes under 1, over 4 and under 3. Call the figure made in this way a cross-over pattern (diagram 2).

Now cross over threads 3 and 4 (diagram 3). Start the 2nd cross-over pattern underneath the first, along the diagonal double knot bar on the left, and do it in the same way as the 1st one (diagram 4).

Next, make the 3rd cross-over pattern and, after that, cross over threads 3 and 4 and work them over the diagonal double knot bar, which, in descending from left to right, will close up the left-hand side of the diamond (diagram 5).

Set apart the next 2 threads, on the bar of knotting which outlines the top right of the diamond, and do a 2nd row of 3 cross-over patterns. Then work a 3rd row of 3 cross-over patterns and close up the last diagonal double knot bar which finishes off the diamond. When you have completed all these diamond shapes in the same way, work a horizontal double knot bar at their base.

Finish off with a picot. These are triangles of rows of diagonal double knots with 3 threads knotted over a leader for each side of the triangle. Each knot incorporates the knotting thread of the 1 before it (see diagram 6). The threads are sewn through and glued behind.

Line the wall light with the white jersey.

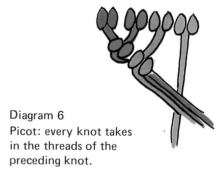

Diagram 6
Picot: every knot takes
in the threads of the
preceding knot.

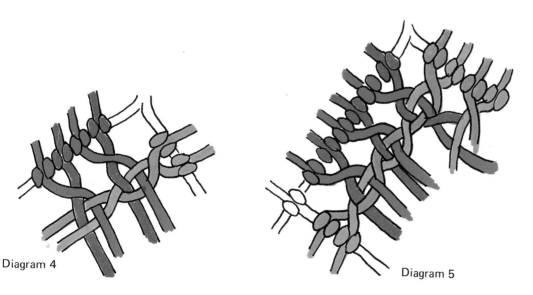

Diagram 4

Diagram 5

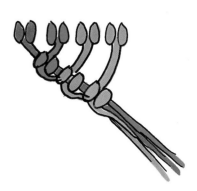

Scented panel

*This decorative mural actually scents
the room in which it hangs by means of
the two little scent bottles attached to it.*

Materials

One thick wooden knitting needle 40 cm
(16 in.) long
6 beads and 2 little bottles or miniature
oriental vases (here they are blue glass)
1 hank of mixed hand-spun wool
12 lengths of natural colored rug wool
25 m (27½ yd) long
18 lengths of 3 mm (1/16 in.) diameter
macramé cotton 25 m (27½ yd)
A few metres (yards) of wool the same color
as the beads and bottles
3 ring-bracelets 7 cm (3 in.) in diameter

Method

Mount the lengths on the wooden thread
bearer as follows:
6 of cotton, 6 of wool, 6 of cotton, 6 of
wool and 6 of cotton.

1st section: After a row of flat knots, make a
windmill (see page 67) with each group of
cotton, followed by a braid of a single
knotted chain at the side, then a plait with
3 strands (10 cm (4 in.) long). Leave the 2
middle threads free. Then repeat the motif
symmetrically in each cotton area.

Between these 3 motifs, put in 4 beads,
held in place with 2 flat knots, 11 cm (4¼ in.)
from the thread bearer and separated from
each other by a 12 cm (4¾ in.) braid of flat
knots.

2nd section: 24 cm (9½ in.) from the thread
bearer, do a row of flat knots, beneath which
you insert 2 beads on 18-19 and 42-43
and hold them in place as above. The 2
threads in the middle become leaders for
diagonal double knot bars with 11 knotting
threads. The groups of cotton at the ends
form an X with bars of double knots, in
which the leaders take the bar of double
knots which starts off from the outside
down to the middle, which lies beneath a
braid of 1 overhand knot and a single knotted
chain of 9 knots. Make a large pea with the
4 central threads, then, beneath the X's at
the sides, 3 columns of flat knots.
With the leaders of the central diagonal
double knot bars, make 2 spirals of vertical
half hitches over 18 and the thread
symmetrical to it.

3rd section: The 1st and last threads return
to the middle as leaders of horizontal bars,
then diagonal double knot bars, in a broken
line. In the middle, the 1st and last cotton
threads become leaders of steeply sloping
diagonal double knot bars and, then join
up again in a braid of 5 flat knots, framed
by vertical half hitches, forming a diamond
shape. On each side, place a ring over which
you knot 14 threads in half hitches, the 1st
and 14th forming a flat knot in its middle.
On either side at the edge make an 11 cm
(4¼ in.) single knotted chain and 4 flat
knots with 4 knotting and 3 core threads.

4th section: The 1st wool thread and the
central cotton thread knotted under the
ring are leaders of diagonal double knot bars,
shaping a leaf (see the photograph) while
the 4 middle threads of the work are made
up into 3 flat knots with double knotting
threads. On the left, work 1 braid of flat
knots, 1 of alternating vertical half hitches,
1 of flat knots, all 6 cm (2½ in.) long. Then,
with the following 3 threads, make 11
alternating vertical half hitches. Repeat on
the right.
In the middle, make a large bead (see the
Glossary) A.

5th section: The wool threads at the sides are
leaders of diagonal double knot bars, which
they take back to the middle. They separate
and return under 6 knotting threads, then
separate again under 8 knotting threads to
outline the bottom of a diamond, in which
you make 8 staggered flat knots.
At the same time, make double diagonal
double knot bars with the 1st wool thread on
the left and the 8th is in cotton, and the

threads on the right of the work symmetrical to them. The 2nd of these rows of knotting lying alongside each other returns towards the middle to cover the top of the diamond before the staggered flat knots are made. Make an overhand knot besides the rows of knotting lying alongside each other over threads 2-3, 5-6-7, 9-10 and those threads symmetrical to them. In the middle, make 6 flat knots, then 3 with double knotting threads.

6th section: Starting from the right: make 1 flat knot 64 cm (25½ in.) from the thread bearer, followed by 6 cm (2½ in.) of half flat knots. Then make a 6 cm (2½ in.) braid of alternating vertical half hitches, from which a diagonal of flat knots, parallel to the left side of the diamond in the 5th section, starts off. At the bottom of this diamond, make a 4.5 cm (1¾ in.) spiral braid of vertical half hitches. In the middle, do 2 bars of curved diagonal double knots, beneath which you add the 3rd ring. The threads covering the ring are separated from each other in the middle and knotted onto the sides at the bottom, thus making the opening where you attach the 1st little bottle of perfume. Repeat the diagonal of flat knots and the curved bar of knotting symmetrically below. Do an overhand knot over 2-3 and 58-59 level with the bottle.

7th section: 4 cm (1½ in.) below this overhand knot, make 5 flat knots at the side and 1 flat knot, *B*, in the middle. With the 1st free thread on the left and the 6th before central *B*, work diagonal double knot bars into a V, joining them up together in a flat knot.
Leave on 1 side the 1st 4 threads on the left and make 3 diagonal bars lying alongside 1 another with the 3 following threads as leaders. In the same way, leave on 1 side the last 4 threads near to the middle and make 3 diagonal double knot bars lying alongside each other. Repeat symmetrically on the right.
On the extreme left of the work, make a braid of 26 alternating vertical half hitches, *C*.
A 4th cotton thread remains free. Use this as leader for a diagonal double knot bar alongside the 3 preceding ones, but having only 4 knotting threads.

8th section: Pass braid *C* in front of the work and use it as a leader over which you work threads for a pyramid (see the *Glossary*). Take up the groups of 4 threads you left on one side. Make a pyramid of 4 knots, the

Design:
Marie-Jeanine SOLVIT

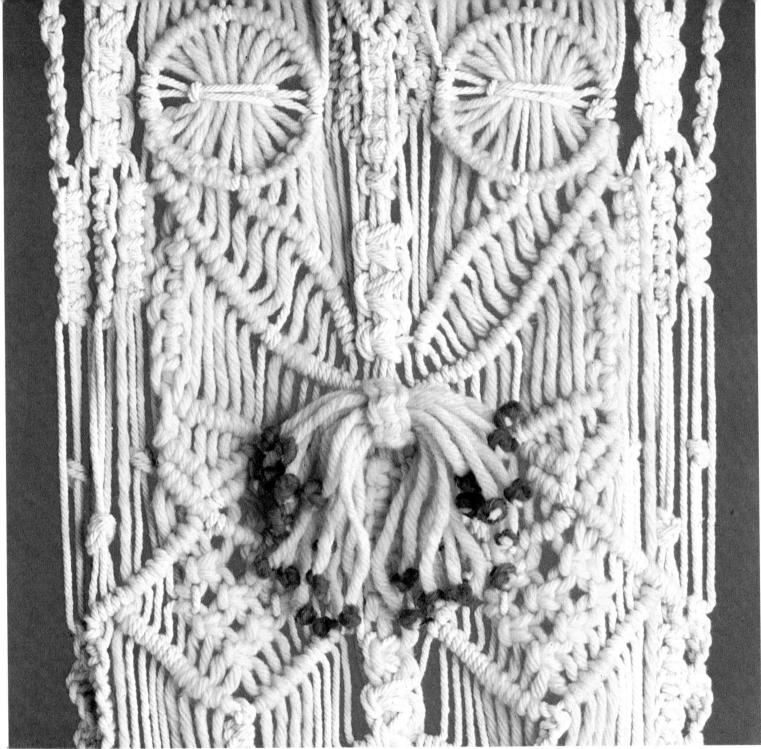

1st being an overhand knot, the 4th a flat knot with 6 core threads. This pyramid stays behind the bars of knotting lying alongside each other in the 6th section. Repeat symmetrically on the right-hand side. Then the triple leader C makes a large flat knot (with 18 core threads), with the 1 symmetrical to it, which you then make up into 2 horizontal braids of a knotted chain of 7 knots, then again becomes leader of a thick bar of horizontal double knots, over which the 1st 6 cotton threads are knotted. Behind, make, with the pyramid threads, 6 flat knots called D and a double chain of 6 knots called E.

9th section: With the 1st 3 free threads on the left, do 47 alternating vertical half hitches.

With the 4th thread as leader, take a diagonal double knot bar from the edge to the middle, using, to work over it, the 1st 10 free threads, then 2 threads from D, 4 core threads from the large central flat knot of the 7th section, then the 4 thteads from E, then the rest of the central threads. Reproduce this symmetrically on the right.

Bind the leader threads in the middle around

the 'waist' of the bottle to hold it at this point.

10th section: The 13th free thread on the left will be leader of a diagonal double knot bar right to left, followed by 2 others lying alongside. The 14th thread leads the 1st 3 diagonal double knot bars, lying alongside each other left-right (over which the 2 threads which were left free at *D* will be knotted). Beneath the 1st 3 bars of knotting lying alongside each other, make a pyramid of 5 flat knots, *F*. Repeat symmetrically on the right. Starting off from the middle, a 1st bar of diagonal double knot moves away, under 13 knotting threads; call these *G*. Next make diagonal double knot bars, which curve around beneath the pyramid, then climb up again to meet the side of the work. Make a large bead in the middle and pass its threads through behind the work before continuing with diagonal double knot bars. The 1st 2 follow the same path as that already made by the 1 above (cross the leaders over in the middle). Then the next 3 spread out in a fan-shape (see the photograph). The 4 threads of the large bead which were passed behind the work come out again above the 2nd bottle and form a 26 cm (10½ in.) braid of half flat knots, the threads of which you darn in behind the work under knot *B*.

11th section: Now, starting from the middle, pass the 1st 8 threads behind the work and bring them out in front again, pulling them through between *F* and *G*. On each side, make a 12 cm (4¾ in.) spiral braid of half flat knots with 6 core threads. These 2 spiral braids are joined up together by binding blue wool around their 12 cm (4¾ in.) length. Cut the hanging threads into lengths graded from 5 to 26 cm (2 to 10½ in.) to make a cluster of 'cocoons' in blue wool. With the 1st 4 free threads near the middle, work 10 cm (4 in.) of half flat knots, ending with a blue cocoon. The 5th thread is leader of a last row of knotting in the fan, beneath which hangs braids of half flat knots of 11, 13, 15 and 15 cm (4¼, 5¼, 5½ and 6 in.) ending in cocoons. Next prepare 15 strands of rug wool graded from 12 to 30 cm (4¾ to 12 in.). Pass them through the big bead *A*. At each end of them, make a very tight double overhand knot in blue wool and cut close. Perhaps it would be wise to secure these delicate knots with a dab of transparent glue. Nothing else remains but to put whatever perfume you choose into the 2 little bottles.

85

Multicolored winged wall-panel

This imposing piece has a Mexican touch.
Put this bright design with marvellous colors on a door;
it is all that is needed to decorate an entrance hall.

Materials

This panel is made in knitting wool with:
175 m (192½ yd) of bright red;
105 m (115½ yd) of purple;
140 m (154 yd) of violet;
105 m (115½ yd) of saffron;
70 m (80 yd) of bright pink
about 1 m (1 yd) greenish-yellow

Method

Mount on a flat wooden thread bearer, 40 cm
(16 in.) long, lengths, each 35 cm (14 in.)
long, as follows:
1 red, 1 purple, 1 violet, 1 red, 1 violet, 1 red,
2 saffron, 1 pink, 1 purple, 1 pink, 1 saffron,
1 red, 1 violet, 1 red, 1 purple, 1 violet.

1st section: Take the 1st thread (left) as
leader of a horizontal double knot bar, which
returns from right to left to make a 2nd

horizontal double knot bar. Then shape a bar
of knots to form 2 semi-circles which rise up
in the middle.
Then the red leader thread drops down 8 cm
(3 in.) on the right and climbs up again in a
diagonal double knot bar to the 8th and 9th
threads after which the bar of knotting
comes down again and stays horizontal from
the 13th to the 20th thread, when it climbs
up again to the 25th and 26th threads and
then comes down again on the right level
with its point of departure.

2nd section: The 11th thread now becomes
leader of a horizontal double knot bar right
to left over which you work all the threads
on the left. Work 8 double knot bars in the
same way, each time taking as leader the 1st
free thread on the right. They change
direction slowly and lean towards the left,
so that the silhouette of the work curves
outwards.

3rd section: The thread bearer of the 8th bar of knotting returns from left to right to make a diagonal double knot bar. Make 6 bars of knotting in the same way, each time taking as leader the 1st free thread on the left. These bars of cording lean more and more to the right. The last knotting thread on the right is a violet thread.

4th section: Continue in the same way with the bars of knotting, always taking the 1st free thread on the left as leader, but finishing the length of the bar each time you knot the violet thread, mentioned at the end of the 3rd section. This decreases their length up to the 7th, over which only 4 threads are knotted.

The leader of the 6th bar of knotting of the 3rd section stays free on the right.

5th section: This thread now follows the inside edge of the 4th section of the work, and all the leaders of this 4th section make vertical half hitches over it. Then, each free thread above this part of the work becomes leader of a bar of vertical knotting, lying alongside the preceding one.
The work is thus shaped on the bias, red 1st, purple next, finally violet. The violet thread makes a half-turn at the point on the right of the work and returns, after it has been knotted over all the vertical threads from right to left.

6th section: After 7 knots in vertical half hitches, this violet thread again becomes leader of a horizontal double knot bar over which the 4 vertical threads on the left are knotted in half hitches. The following threads, to the right of this section of the work on the bias, do the same. This results in 7 bars of knotting, at 1st horizontal, then gradually leaning over towards the left in a fan-shape. Leave this left-hand part of the work on 1 side and repeat symmetrically on the right.

7th section: Go back up to the point where the saffron threads were left on 1 side. With them, make a 10 cm (4 in.) braid of half flat knots. Do the same with the pink and saffron threads lying to the right of the pink and purple threads in the middle.

8th section: 4 threads remain in the middle: 2 pink and 2 purple. Make an overhand knot with the 1st and the 3rd, and an overhand knot with the 2nd and the 4th, doing this 4 cm (1½ in.) below the horizontal double

Design:
Odette SANSONNET

87

knot bar above. Then, 32 cm (12¾ in.) lower down, make an overhand knot with 1 pink and 1 purple, leaving free 1 purple thread on the left and 1 pink thread on the right. Then make 1 overhand knot with the 4 threads 2 cm (¾ in.) lower down.

9th section: Still on the central motif, use the 1st thread on the left as leader of a diagonal double knot bar left to right, over which you work 5 threads. The leader thread makes a half-turn to climb up and lead a bar of knotting parallel to the preceding one. Then this same leader falls free and, 4 cm (1½ in.) lower down, it goes back towards the middle in a diagonal double knot bar left to right. Next, follow the same steps as those in sections 4, 5, 6. The number of working threads is much less and the triangle, turned towards the inside, will be saffron, edged with purple on the left. There are then 4 bars of knotting which get narrower, then 4 which widen out. The leader thread of the last 1 then forms a diagonal double knot bar, going down from left to right, and then setting off again from right to left.

10th section: Repeat the work done in the 9th section symmetrically on the right side of the work.

11th section: In the middle, the purple makes 2 half hitches over the pink, on the bias, then over the 2nd purple on the right. Then the pink thread next to the 4 1st saffron makes 2 half hitches over the pink, then over the purple on the right. Next the purple thread on the right does 2 half hitches over the 2 pink threads lying to its left.

12th section: Still in the middle, the 1st saffron thread on the left is leader of a bar of knotting which curves in an oval shape beneath the knots of the 11th section. At either end of this oval (the longest diameter of which is horizontal), is a saffron thread.

13th section: Taking the saffron thread to the left of the oval as leader, make a diagonal double knot bar parallel to the last bar of knotting left on 1 side at the left of the work.
Work 2 bars of double knots below this 1, taking as leaders the 2 following saffron threads. Work 3 symmetrical bars of knots to the right of the work.

14th section: The 2 threads remaining in the middle are knotted together into an overhand knot 4 cm (1½ in.) below the central oval. Then the 4 pink and purple threads in the middle split up, 2 to the right, 2 to the left, pass on either side of the central oval, then pass behind the 3 leaders of the bars of knots. With 1 pink thread on the left of and one purple thread on the right of the middle threads, do 4 half flat knots over these. Leave this part of the work to 1 side.

15th section: The next to last knotting thread, to the right of the last diagonal double knot bar on the left-hand side of the work, falls freely for 6 cm (2½ in.) then becomes leader of a horizontal double knot bar right to left, which turns on the left of the work to return from left to right, 2 cm (¾ in.) lower down, forming the shape of a sloping leaf. Then the leader returns from right to left in a horizontal double knot bar.
Repeat symmetrically on the right-hand side of the work.

16th section: Take up where you left off at the bottom of the 14th section, and make a cross-over with bars of knotting, taking as leaders the last knotting threads (on either side of the middle of the last diagonal double knot bar in the 13th section over which the 6 threads from the middle of the work will work.

17th section: Then these leaders make diagonal double knot bars which move away from each other at the middle towards the outside. 15 threads work over each.

18th section: Continue on the left with 4 bars of knotting underneath the 1st one. The 1st of these 4 bars of double knots has as leader the purple thread in the middle. The 3 following take as leader the 1st free thread on the right.
Repeat symmetrically on the right of the work.

19th section: The pink thread, then the saffron thread in the middle become leaders of the 2 following bars of knotting. On the right of the work, these 2 leaders are: the purple, then the pink.

20th section: Do the same work on the bias as for the triangles you have already done higher up, with vertical bars of knotting, using leaders from the 17th and 18th sections. You end with a saffron point on the left, the knotting thread of which returns towards the middle in vertical half hitches over all the return threads to then become leader of a new horizontal double knot bar. Then the pink thread below does the same work before it becomes free again at the middle of the panel.
Repeat symmetrically on the right. This time, a purple thread is free again in the middle.

21st section: After the violet thread at the base of the triangle has made 5 vertical half hitches, it becomes leader of a diagonal double knot bar, which is crossed over in the middle by its symmetrical thread from the right. Then this same leader makes 2 horizontal double knot bars over which only 12 threads work. And it starts off again, crossing over its symmetrical thread in the middle, in 2 gently sloping bars of diagonal knotting, curving around at the ends to return and cross over again in the middle. Then make a small diamond, over which 5 threads work from each side. Then the leaders cross over each other again and work down on the bias in vertical half hitches over 5 threads on each side. Once again, you make triangles in the same way as higher up. But, the horizontal thread which marks the middle of this triangle continued towards the outside, where it continues as leader of 3 successive horizontal double knot bars, 8 threads working over each of them.

22nd section: The violet threads which made the half hitches marking the top of the triangle come out again beneath the latter on the right and left in 5th position. They return to make vertical half hitches over the next 4 threads, then cross over each other in the middle and continue with 2 rows of vertical half hitches (there and back) over these 4 same threads. Then these 4 threads become leaders, 1st of all of horizontal knots, then gradually of diagonal double knot bars (in a fan shape). Work 7 threads over the 1st, then 8 over the 2nd, 9 over the 3rd and 10 over the 4th. The 5th will have the violet thread near the middle as leader. Then, 7 diagonal double knot bars lying alongside each other follow, each taking as leader the 1st free thread on the right for that on the left, on the left for that on the right. Cross over in rellis patter (see the *Glossary*) 3 threads from each side in the middle.

23rd section: An oval hole has been formed in the middle of the work. The threads which were left free on either side of the diamond in the 21st section, now pass behind the work to come out again through this oval hole.

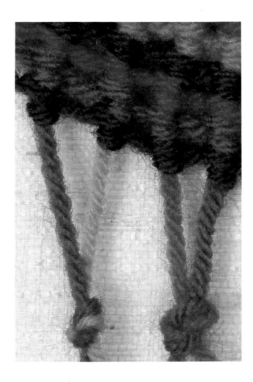

They are bound around for 8 cm (3 in.) with a light greenish-yellow thread. They hang in front of the work and are finished off with round balls of wool in different sizes, their shapes held by matching threads which are almost invisible. Look at the photograph to see how the balls are arranged.

24th section: The 1st free thread on the left of the left half of the work now becomes a vertical leader, over which you work all the threads of this half in vertical half hitches. Each free thread above the vertical knotting in its turn becomes leader for a row of knotting lying alongside the preceding one. The work of all the threads gives 12 rows of knots, the last of which is covered by only 2 half hitches of a single knotting thread. Repeat this work symmetrically on the right. These 2 'wings' which stick out on the right and left must be held out at each end with a little nail. Knot the threads in 2s into 2 rows of alternating overhand knots. Finish with round balls of wool like those in the middle, varying in length between 55 and 80 cm (22 and 32 in.) below the last knots. The colors for this work were not mounted quite symmetrically, so that on 1 side the work varies a little.

Doormat

The sunny color of baling twine
makes this a bright and cheerful mat.
The attractive design is also lively
and makes the mat suitable for use as a wall
hanging too.
The size of the mat is 70 x 50 cm. (28 x 20 in.).

Materials

About 315 m (340½ yd) of baling twine.
14.40 m (16 yd) for the leader which goes
all around the perimeter of the doormat
75 double lengths of 2 m (2¼ yd), (that is,
150 lengths mounted double)

Method

Mark the corners of a 70 x 50 cm (28 x
20 in.) rectangle with nails onto a knotting
board. Form the perimeter-leader of the
doormat by taking 6 threads around the
surface marked out in this way (see the
photograph). Then mount 24 double threads
in reverse lark's head knots on side B—C.
You work vertically and horizontally at the
same time. The 10th thread of B—C is leader
of a bar of knotting, then the 24th, the 28th
and the 35th.
Follow the diagram to shape the rows of
knots, between which the threads work

Design: Odile TRENTESAUX

perpendicularly in a left to right direction.
Notice that, on side B—D, the threads are
not mounted an equal distance apart. After
the 4th, there is an empty space, followed by
a length which shapes the little triangle on
the left, the leaders of which follow the path
E—F—G. The threads of the 3 lengths
mounted between E and G are worked very
loosely into half hitches to decorate the
whole area of this triangle.
The same technique is used to fill the area
lying above side D—A. The lengths mounted
on B—C (24) and the lengths mounted on
D—A (28) end their path over leader H—I,
each thread being laid along the leader at
the bottom and covered over by the half
hitches which make the row of knotting.
If you follow the diagram enlarged on graph
paper, you can work out the directions
taken to make the design. The twin bar of
knotting lying above H—I has a single thread
as leader, over which you pull the half
hitches tight.
The charm of this piece lies in the irregularity
of the knotting. The half hitches are
alternatively tight and loose; they are made
over 1, 2, 4 or 6-stranded leaders.

Beaded pendant necklace

*You can wear this necklace
with a solid-colored blouse or dress.
The bold design shows up best. This
necklace makes even the simplest clothes look original.*

Materials

138 round natural colored wooden beads, 4 mm (1/8 in.) in diameter
fine knitting cotton: 2 violet lengths 6.60 m (7¼ yd) long, 2 light blue lengths 6.60 m (7¼ yd) long, 4 light blue lengths 2.80 m (3 yd) long, 4 medium blue lengths 2.80 m (3 yd) long, 2 navy blue lengths 2.80 m (3 yd) long; this is for starting off the work
12 violet lengths 0.70 m (1 yd) long, which you will add on in the course of the work

Method

You have 2 violet lengths 6.60 m (7¼ yd) long and 2 light blue lengths 6.60 m (7¼ yd) long, all the rest being much shorter. Take a knotting board and pin all the threads out on it through their respective middles in the following order: a first group with: 1 violet 6.60 m (7¼ yd) long, 2 light blue, 2 medium blue and 1 navy blue 2.80 m (3 yd) long, then 1 light blue 6.60 m (7¼ yd) long.
Lay out the 2nd group in the same way.
In each group, the long threads on the outsides will mask the other 5 by making vertical half hitches over them in 3s. In other words do * 3 violet half hitches, 3 light blue half hitches * 4 times from * to *, which gives you 8 half hitches in alternate colors. Then tie all the threads from the 2 groups tightly together in a violet flat knot. Again, work 8 groups of vertical half hitches and 1 violet flat knot. Repeat these motifs 10 times in all to form large links of a chain.

Then turn the knotting board around, make a violet flat knot (which is the half-way point around the neck) and again make 10 links of a chain like those symmetrical to them. The chain of the necklace is now finished.
Pin the 2 ends side by side — that is, 2 violet flat knots. Starting from the left, leave 1 light blue thread free, then make a single knotted chain of 4 knots with 1 violet and 1 light blue, then with 2 medium blue, 2 navy blue, 2 light blue, 2 medium blue, 2 light blue and in the middle with 1 violet from each group.
Repeat symmetrically on the right. The thread you left free becomes leader of a horizontal double knot bar. Where the bars of knotting meet up in the middle, they

are joined together in an overhand knot, and again make 2 bars of knotting lying alongside the preceding 1. When they meet in the middle, they become central threads of 6 alternating vertical half hitches. Level with them on the left, do 4 overhand knots over the 1st thread (violet). Then thread on 2 beads, each followed by an overhand knot. Then continue threading on the beads, 1 onto each thread, and stagger them. Finish with an overhand knot under each.

Each thread nearest the middle then becomes in turn leader of a horizontal double knot bar. Work 8 bars of knots in this way, inclining them slightly towards the left side. Repeat symmetrically on the right.

The leader of the last bar of knots remains free at the outside. Insert 1 bead on thread 2, 2 on thread 4, 3 on thread 6, 4 on thread 8, 3 on thread 10, 2 on thread 12, and 2 on the last thread, each bead being followed by an overhand knot. The 1st thread on the left is leader of a curved bar knots which underlines this beaded motif. On this bar, after the knotting of the 4th thread (light blue), add 2 violet lengths, each 0.70 m (1 yd) long. Knot the 5 following threads and again add 2 violet lengths. Return in the opposite direction with the same leaders and again add 2 violet lengths at the left-hand side.

Now start off again from the right, where a navy blue thread is leader. Make 3 bars of knots lying alongside in the same way, taking the 1st thread on the right as leader. Insert a bead, followed by an overhand knot, onto the 1st 5 threads on the left. Then add a bead preceded by an overhand knot on thread 6 and thread 8; on thread 7, the knot which precedes the bead is 0.5 cm (1/8 in.) lower down. Place a bead, followed by an overhand knot on threads: 10, 12, 14, 16, 18, 20, 22, 24, 26. On threads 9, 11, 23 and 25, place the beads a little lower down so that they fall into a staggered position. Put 2 beads onto thread 22. Then put 3 beads onto threads 13 and 21. And 4 beads onto threads 15, 17 and 19. All are followed by an overhand knot. Repeat symmetrically on the right and cut close under each of the last overhand knots.

Design:
Marie-Jeanine SOLVIT

Place mat with knife rest

Three plain wooden beads have been added to this place-mat
to form a knife rest.
You can wipe them clean with a sponge.
They won't be harmed when you wash the place-mat, which
is made of pure cotton.
The meandering bars of knotting
make room for a plate and glass
and form separate areas decorated by different types of knots.
It measures 30 x 45 cm (12 x 18 in.).

Materials

About 188 m (210 yd) of macramé cotton,
2 mm (1/16 in.) in diameter: 78 lengths each
2.40 m (2¾ yd) long, plus 1 thread 4.55 m
(5 yd) long
3 large wooden beads

Method

Keep back 2.30 m (2½ yd) on your 4.55 m
(5 yd) thread. These 2.30 m (2½ yd) will be
to the left of the leader thread, pinned along
45 cm (18 in.) of the knotting board. On the
right, a 1.80 m (2 yd) length hangs free.
Mount the 78 lengths in reverse lark's head
knots on the 45 cm (18 in.) leader. On the
right, start off the diagonal double knot bar
right to left with the 1st 4 threads. Then
make flat knots in the 1st section, but without
using the 1st 4 threads on the left, as you
knot these over the row of knotting left to
right.
Continue the flat knots, filling in the surfaces
lying above the 1st row of knotting, following
the diagram, which you should enlarge on
squared paper and placed on the knotting
board so that you can follow the design
by working directly over it.
The areas are numbered.

In area 1, make a flat knot with 2 knotting
threads over 13 core threads. At the edge,
on the right at point A, make half hitches

Design: Marie-Jeanine SOLVIT

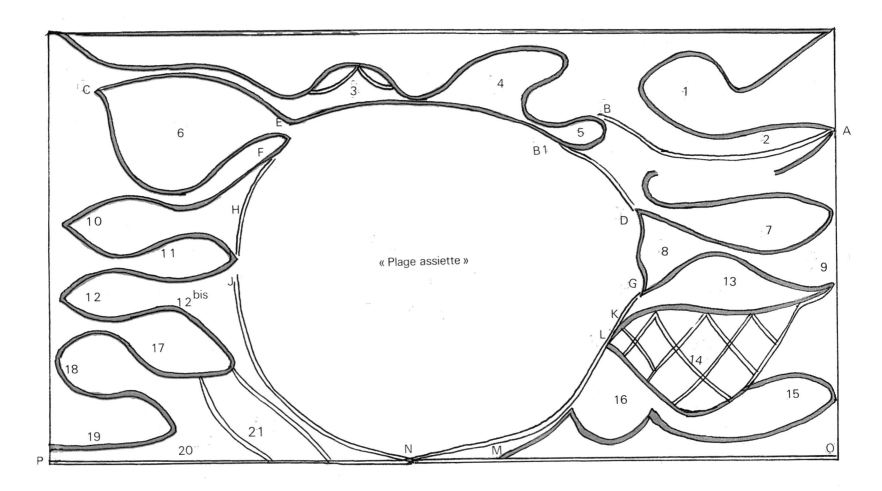

« Plage assiette »

to cover the curved part of the row of knotting, with the left-hand thread of the flat knot on the border, to make a connection. While you knot the left-hand thread of this flat knot over the bar of knots, the leader thread of the row of knots becomes the left-hand knotting thread of the flat knot on this row.

The row of cording underlining **area 2** takes as leader a knotting thread that is right there and the leader which wound around from the top right-hand corner of the work picks up its path again from point A. Fill area 2 with single knotted chains.

Now start on the row of knotting left to right, on the left of the work; its leader is the 2.30 (2½ yd) thread kept back on the left of the thread bearer.

It underlines the flat knot motifs above and moves along to join up with the other bar of knots at point B, after 1st rounding area 3 which is decorated with 2 bars of double knots, above a large overhand knot with 8 threads, and then **area 4**, in which you make double knotted chains.

Where the line meets point B, it turns, encircling a flat knot (11 threads between 2 knotting threads) of **area 5**. It starts off again towards the left, following the upper contour of the plate, then moves up again.

Come down again from point C after working in vertical half hitches (in groups of 3 hitches over 2 middle threads right to left, left to right), the inside of this **area 6**, the space for the glass on the mat. Leave that part for the moment and continue again the bar of

knotting which starts off from point A. Knot 9 threads over the leader, then thread the leader through 3 wooden beads, beneath which 22 threads hang free. Follow the diagram.

The threads reappearing beneath the beads work over the leader which starts off from the left-hand bead towards the right-hand side and outlines **area 7**, which is decorated with vertical alternating half hitches over 2 central threads.

At the same time, work the edge of the place-mat in alternating flat knots. Point D closes up area 7.

Now make a start on the braids of flat knots which fill up the plate area. They consist of 4 flat knots, but those on the 1st row, following around the curve of the bar of

96

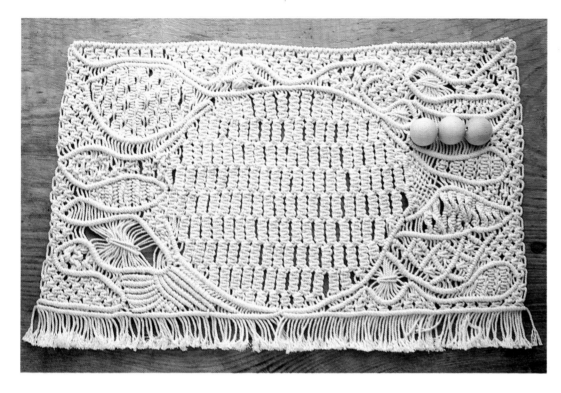

From H to I, a few vertical half hitches start off the 4th row of the central braids. Then the surface of **area 11** is striped with braids of vertical half hitches left to right and right to left alternately (the braids face, then turn their backs on each other).

Area 12 relies only on its vertical threads which are left unworked. This area (see 12a) also has a triangle of alternating flat knots. A spare knotting thread is the leader, starting off from point J, beneath the 5th row of the central braids.

Begin the work again on the right-hand side to form **area 13** in which vertical half hitches spiral in longer or shorter lengths depending on their position.

In **area 14**, make diagonal knot bars in diamond shapes with flat knots in the middle. From point L to point M, a spare knotting thread underlines area 14 and shapes **area 15** (filled with alternating vertical half hitches with 2 knotting threads over 2 core threads, 3 times) and **area 16** which is filled with 1 flat knot with 2 knotting threads over 13 core threads.

Finish off the central area (a total of 8 alternating rows of braids plus a last row at the bottom with groups of flat knots in this order: 1, 2, 2, 2, 2, 2, 1) to fit into the curve J-N and L-N.

Make a few alternating flat knots beneath **area 15 and 16**, and continue the bar of knotting J-N horizontally to end its path at point O.

Return to the left. **Area 17** has 1 large flat knot with 2 knotting threads over 23 core threads.

In **area 18**, make 3 double knotted chains (from left to right: 4 knots, 5 and 2). The area around the border continues in alternating flat knots which fill out **area 19**.

Finally, work **area 20** in bars of knots which are more or less horizontal. **Area 21** is composed of 5 parallel diagonal double knot bars. The leader L-N continues on horizontally up to the last point at P.

Leave a short 4 cm (1½ in.) fringe at the bottom of the place-mat and untwist the threads.

You might want to make several place-mats. Try to keep the same lay-out for the plate area and area 6, where the glass goes, and also for the 3-bead knofe-holder, but vary the path of the leader threads throughout to form different shaped areas. Alter the knots so that all the place-mats in the same set are different. Anyone who uses these mats will have a 'personalized' design.

knotting, has, from left to right: 3 knots, then 3, 3, 3, 4, 4, 4, 4, 4, 4, 4, 4, 3, 2 and 1 flat knot.

Then go down a little in a diagonal double knot bar from point E to point F and on the right do a bar of knots from B to D, using as leader a knotting thread that is right there. After this, do the 2nd row of braids in the plate area.

Note: beneath point E, on the extreme left of the 1st row of flat knots, is 1 flat knot, level with the bottom knot of the braids and, beneath point F, on the extreme left of the 2nd row, are 2 flat knots, level with the base of the braids.

On the left of these 2 flat knots, a nearby knotting thread becomes leader of 5 knotting threads and becomes the left-hand knotting

thread of the 2 flat knots which start off the 3rd row of braids in the central area (at point H).

Now outline **area B**.

It has a trellis-pattern middle, (see the *Glossary*), the threads of which work in vertical half hitches over the row of knots between D and G.

Area 9 contains staggered overhand knots. Two alternating flat knots provide the border on the right of the mat.

Leave this to go to work on **area 10** in which you make special alternating flat knots: between the 2 parts of the knot, add an overhand knot which juts out over the sides of each of the flat knots.

Room divider with ceramic beads

This splendid design is easy to make.
It measures 0.82 x 2.12 m (1 x 2.1/3 yd).

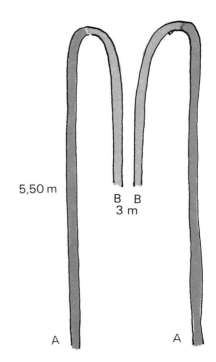

Materials

1 wooden rod 0.82 m (1 yd) long
495 m (545 yd) of string: 54 lengths, each
8.50 m (9.1/3 yd) long
81 ceramic beads

Method

Mount the string on a wooden rod 0.82 cm
(1 yd) long. To do this, prepare lengths
8.50 m, (9.1/3 yd) long, divided as follows:
Instead of folding the lengths into 2 equal
parts, fold them so that 1 side is 3 m

(3.1/3 yd) long, the other 5.50 m (6 yd). Mount
the lengths, laying them out symmetrically
in this way: call the 5.50 m (6 yd) thread A
and the 3 m (3.1/3 yd) thread B. The
mounting will be: ABBA, ABBA, ABBA,
and so on, so that the 2 threads of 3 m
(3.1/3 yd) are always framed by the 2
threads of 5.50 m (6 yd), with which the
flat knots will be made.
Mount 54 lengths AB as described above, in
double lark's head knots (pass the 2 central
threads twice into the loop. Knot behind).
Next work a horizontal double knot bar
over a leader thread made up of 4 threads

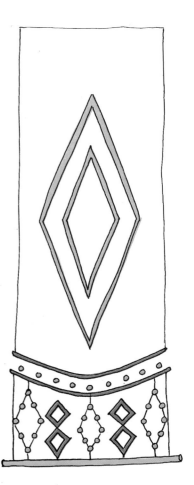

cut a little longer than the length of the wooden rod and finished off at either end by a double knot. There are 108 working threads.

1st row: Form a flat knot with threads 9, 10, 11, 12 (10 and 11 are the fillers, 9 and 12 form the flat knot); then 31, 32, 33, 34; next 53, 54, 55, 56; then 75, 76, 77, 78; finally: 97, 98, 99, 100.

2nd row: Make a flat knot under the 1st (9 and 12); flat knot with 29, 32; flat knot with 33, 36; flat knot with 53, 56; flat knot with 73, 76 and 77, 80; flat knot with 97, 100. Divide the work into 5 groups of threads as follows:
20 threads, 24 threads, 20 threads (central motif), 24 threads and 20 threads.
The 1st, 3rd and 5th groups are identical.

1st group: Thread 1 bead through the 2 core threads of the central flat knot, hold in place with 2 consecutive flat knots. On the following 2 rows, make 2 consecutive flat knots, slanted towards the right and towards the left, made up of 2 threads from the preceding flat knot and 2 adjacent threads. Start on the next 2 rows, again jutting out by 2 threads. The core threads will be 6, 7 and 14, 15. Add a bead on these core threads, held in place by 2 consecutive flat knots.
Continue in the same way up to the point where you make 2 consecutive flat knots with the side threads of the motif. Add a bead on the central threads (2, 3 and 18, 19). Level with these 2 beads, make a flat knot with 7, 8 and 13, 14, the core threads of which are made up by 9, 10, 11, 12. Beneath the 2 beads you have put in like this at the side and which are held in place with 2 consecutive flat knots, continue working flat knots on the bias, symmetrically with those described above, so that you insert 2 beads onto core threads 6, 7 and 14, 15, then 1 bead onto the core threads 10, 11, which are held in place with 2 consecutive flat knots. Repeat this motif in the 3rd and 5th groups of working threads. Between these groups, continue with the flat knots on the bias to form the design of groups 2 and 4:

Group 2: *Make a total of 6 flat knots on the bias towards the outside edges of the group of threads, the 6th made with lateral threads: 1, 3 and 21, 24. Do the same again, this time returning towards the middle marked by the flat knot 11, 14*. Repeat from

* to *. Do group 4 in the same way.
Next make a bar of curved knotting right across the work in the shape of a circular arc (see the photograph) with a leader of 4 threads, finished off with a double knot at either end.
Then, taking groups of 4 threads, alternate spiral braids of half flat knots (threads 1, 4 over middle 2, 3) and motifs with a bead framed by 2 flat knots.
Do 1 beaded motif (with the bead in the middle) 2 spiral braids, 1 beaded, 2 spiral braids, and so on, with a spiral braid at either end. Then repeat the horizontal double knot bar to frame this decorative strip, as the photograph shows.
Then, taking the threads in groups of 4, make groups of 2 consecutive flat knots 10 cm (4 in.) from the bar of knots lying above them. Repeat these groups of 2 consecutive flat knots every 7 cm (3 in.) right down to the bottom of the room divider, making, in the middle of the work, a decorative beaded motif in the shape of a double diamond, each bead being framed by 2 consecutive flat knots above and below it.
There are 27 groups of 4 threads.
The instructions given are for the right-hand side of the work, which you repeat symmetrically.

Large diamond:
1 bead on group 14;
1 bead 7 cm (3 in.) lower down on 15;
1 bead 10 cm (4 in.) lower down on 16;
1 bead 10 cm (4 in.) lower down on 17;
1 bead 5 cm (2 in.) lower down on 18;
1 bead 5 cm (2 in.) lower down on 19;
1 bead 7 cm (3 in.) lower down on 20;
1 bead 5 cm (2 in.) lower down on 21;
1 bead 7 cm (3 in.) lower down on 22
Do the same work symmetrically to bring you back towards the middle of the diamond.

Small diamond in the middle: 1 bead on group 14, 32 cm (12¾ in.) lower down than the 1st.
Then 1 bead 8 cm (3 in.) lower down on 15
1 bead 9 cm (3¼ in.) lower down on 16
1 bead 9 cm (3¼ in.) lower down on 17
1 bead 5 cm (2 in.) lower down on 18
and return symmetrically down to the bottom of the small diamond with a central bead on 14.
The last group of 2 consecutive flat knots lie 194 cm (77½ in.) from the thread bearer.
Cut the threads off at a total finished length of 212 cm (about 85 in.). You can change this length to suit your needs.

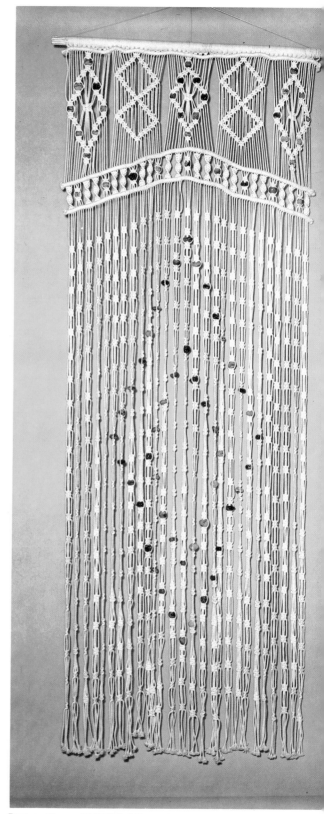

Design: Maryse DUBOULOIS

Large blue and green lampshade

Here is how to make an illuminated forest hanging.

Materials

1 lampshade frame with the top ring 12 cm
(4¾ in.) in diameter; bottom ring 60 cm
(24 in.) in diameter, height of the frame
26 cm (10 in.); and 16 support struts
2 plain rings to add in the course of the work
340 m (374 yd) of sky blue cotton
306 m (337 yd) of bright blue cotton
142 m (156 yd) of green cotton

Method

The cottons used here were dyed by the
maker of the project. When making this
lampshade, you can, of course, harmonize
the colors to fit in with your décor.
The hanging cords consist of 4 sky blue
spiral braids, made with half flat knots, with
8 lengths, each 3.20 m (3½ yd). Proceed as
follows:
Mount 2 spiral braids by straddling 2 threads
for each braid over the top metal ring;
26 cm (10 in.) from the start, make the
hanging loop (11 cm (4¼ in.) long, doubled over)
and continue the 2 spiral braids for 26 cm
(10 in.). Then attach the ends equidistant
from the 1st 2 on the ring and secure them

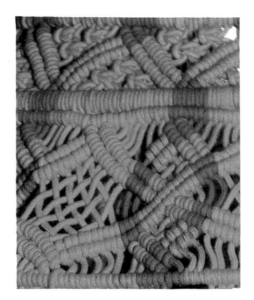

Design: Maryse DUBOULOIS

with 2 half hitch knots, strengthened with
transparent glue.

Body of the lampshade

Mount 32 lengths, each 8 m (9 yd) long, in
reverse lark's head knots in bright blue.
Make double diagonal double knot bars into
8 diamonds, putting a flat knot of 6 threads
(4 core threads) in the middle.
There are 6 threads between the leader
threads of the 1st row of the descending
diagonal double knot bars.

1st row: Make 4 half hitches over the leader
thread left to right, but 3 half hitches over
the leader thread right to left.

2nd row: the bar of knotting right to left
continues at the junction, to be covered
by 9 successive half hitches. Make the 2
half hitches lying on either side of the central
flat knot with inserted lengths to increase the
fullness of the work which flares out following the shape of the frame (add lengths of
7.50 m (8¼ yd).
Now go back to the 12 threads beneath each
of the completed diamonds. With threads
3, 4, 5, 6 and 7, 8, 9, 10, make a knot of a
double chain 4 times. Use threads 1 and
2, 11 and 12 for joining up with threads 11
and 12 and 1 and 2 of the adjacent diamonds
and form a knot of a double chain 5 times.

At the bottom of the braids of double knotted chain — there are 24 all around the work — insert a metal ring (ring of a lampshade) to take the place of a leader thread. Cover it beforehand with adhesive cotton tape to give it extra thickness. Cover this rigid ring in the same way as a normal horizontal double knot bar with the threads of the spiral braids. Between each group of 4 lengths (8 threads over the leader), mount a 7.50 m (8¼ yd) sky blue length in a reverse lark's head knot. In this way, you alternate * 8 bright blue threads, 2 sky blue threads *, and so on, from * to *. Immediately below this thick bar of horizontal knots, do a 2nd horizontal double knot bar with a single-thread leader in the same cotton as that used for the rest of the work.

Starting with a group of 4 bright blue lengths (8 threads), made up from those on the preceding row, work 2 sky blue half hitches with the 2 threads from the preceding row. Add 2 sky blue lengths mounted in reverse lark's head knots (this adds 8 sky blue threads of 7.50 m (8¼ yd) onto the leader thread), then the 2 half hitches with the 2 sky blue threads of the preceding row, while the 4 bright blue threads from the preceding row hang on the inside of the lampshade.

About 13 cm (5 in.) from the starting point, these threads form a spiral braid of half flat knots, 38 cm (15 in.) long, giving a total length of 51 cm (20 in.) to these 12 spiral braids which will hang around the electric light bulb on the inside of the lampshade.

When you have completed the horizontal double knot bar, make 2 flat knots with the groups of 8 sky blue threads, then, staggered between them, a central flat knot. Between these sky blue flat knots, there are groups of 4 bright blue threads. With the 2 threads on the left, make a diagonal double knot bar left to right, the 1st 2 half hitches of which will be made with the 2 bright blue threads on the right. These will then act as leaders for 2 diagonal double knot bars right to left, covered by:
1) the 4 sky blue threads from the adjacent staggered flat knots on the left, then
2) 2 sky blue lengths added to increase the size of the work;
3) 2 bright blue half hitches made with the 2 leader threads of the diagonal double knot bars left to right of the adjacent motif on the left.

The diagonal double knot bars left to right are covered with 2 bright blue half hitches, then 4 sky blue half hitches with the threads of the adjacent staggered flat knots on the right, followed by 2 sky blue lengths added in the same way as on the bar of knotting right to left.

With the 12 sky blue threads which are hanging between the diagonal double knot bars, do 3 rows of staggered flat knots — that is, 1 flat knot on the 1st row 2 on the 2nd row and 3 on the 3rd row.

Repeat the technique used for the metal ring added above (but with a bigger ring, since the shape of the frame is widening out) and use it as a leader for a horizontal double knot bar.

You should have: * 4 bright blue half hitches, 2 sky blue half hitches, 1 green half hitch, using an inserted length, 8 sky blue half hitches with the 8 sky blue threads from the preceding row, 1 green half hitch with an inserted thread, 2 sky blue half hitches.* Repeat from * to * all the way around.

The groups of 8 sky blue threads are left hanging on the inside. Work them, after 5 cm (2 in.), into spiral braids of half flat knots 33 cm (13¼ in.) long — 38 cm (15 in.) total length.

Make another horizontal double knot bar cording as above with a single thread, over which you work, starting with a group of bright blue threads: *4 bright blue half hitches, 2 sky blue half hitches, 2 green half hitches, 1 green half hitch with an inserted length, 1 green double half hitch with an inserted length, 1 green half hitch with an inserted length, 2 green half hitches, 2 sky-blue half hitches*. Repeat from * to * all around.

Do 2 diagonal double knot bars in green as follows: there are 16 green threads on the horizontal leader from which 10 threads hang down. Use the 4th thread as leader for a diagonal double knot bar left to right. The 5th thread acts as leader for a diagonal double knot bar left to right parallel to the 1st. It will cover by 5 half hitches made by threads 6, 7, 8, 9 and 10, then by a 6th half hitch made with an inserted green thread.

After thread 6 has made a half hitch over leader 5 and a half hitch over leader 4, it will itself act as leader for the diagonal double knot bar right to left above, while the leader of the diagonal double knot bar right to left below will be thread 7. On the upper diagonal right to left, make 3 half hitches with threads 1, 2, 3. and add a green length in a half hitch to the left of the half hitch of thread 1. This gives you 5 half hitches on the lower diagonal right to left. On the upper diagonal left ro right you have 5 half hitches plus 1 half hitch with an inserted length. On the lower diagonal left to right you have 7 half hitches. These green diagonal double knot bars see their leaders continue down to the base of the frame to form the symmetrical figure at the bottom of the work. The middle of the green diamond formed in this way is a trellis (see the Glossary) made with 10 threads.

The 2-tone blue motif lying between the green ones starts off from the thin horizontal double knot bar with 2 sky blue threads, 4 bright blue threads 2 sky blue threads — 8 threads in all.

The 3rd and 4th are leaders of 2 diagonal double knot bars left to right, over which you make 3 half hitches with threads 5 and 6. Then these 2 threads form the 2 diagonal double knot bars right to left, covered with 2 sky blue half hitches made with threads 1 and 2, while threads 7 and 8 make half hitches over the diagonal double knot bars left to right, using 3 and 4 as leaders.

Do a little trellis pattern with 4 sky blue threads. Then leaders 3 and 4 make 2 half hitches over the green bar of diagonal knots from the adjacent motif on the left, followed by 2 sky blue half hitches with threads 7 and 8. Symmetrically, over the green bar of diagonal knots from the adjacent motif on the right, make 2 bright blue half hitches with threads 3 and 4, and 2 sky blue half hitches with threads 1 and 2.

At the cross-over, which marks the middle of this design, make 2 green half hitches over each green leader of the diagonal double knot bar right to left.

Threads 5, 6, 7 and 8 continue this double diagonal double knot bar right to left, and so do, symmetrically, threads 1, 2, 3 and 4 over the diagonal double knot bar left to right.

Then, the 4 sky blue threads from the trellis in the middle pass in sky blue half hitches over leaders 5 and 6 on the left, 3 and 4 on the right. This oval motif in 2-tone blue with a green middle is completed with 4 bright blue half hitches made with 3 and 4 over leaders 5 and 6. Attach all the blue threads at the bottom of the frame with half hitches, strengthened by transparent glue.

Each of the green motifs finishes with 14 threads: 1, 2, 3 and 4 do a half hitch over the metal of the frame. Then you work them into a 17 cm (7 in.) long spiral braid of half flat knots.

The same applies to threads 5, 6, 7 and 8: between 9 and 10, insert a green length, called 9a and 10a. In this way, you get 4 green threads with which you make the 3rd spiral braid of half flat knots.

Work threads 11, 12, 13 and 14 in the same way, so that you have a total of 4 braids hanging under each pale green motif of the lampshade, which is now finished. Don't use a high powered electric light bulb. Bright lights get very hot and can cause a fire.

Cylindrical parcel string lampshade

Design: Maryse DUBOULOIS

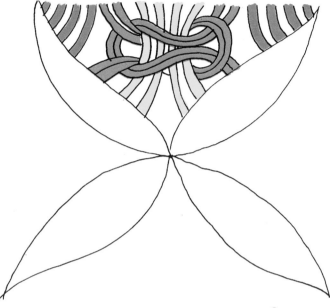

1 2 3 4 5 6   7 8   9 10 11 12 13 14 15 16

One complete section
with threads numbered
for easy reference.

Material

A cylindrical frame 30 cm (12 in.) in diameter
and 44 cm (17½ in.) high with 8 equidistant
vertical support struts between the rings
About 282 m (300 yd) parcel string

Method

In each of the gaps between the struts, mount
8 lengths — 64 lengths in all. Make each
length 10 times the height of the frame —
about 4.40 m (5 yd) and is used folded in 2.
Take as thread bearer the bottom ring of the
lampshade. The row on which you finish
off — which will probably not be quite so
neat — will be on top (the end which you
cannot see too clearly).
For each 1/8th of the lampshade:
starting from the left: make 1 lark's head
knot (loop behind);

1 double lark's head knot;
1 lark's head knot;
1 double lark's head knot;
1 lark's head knot;
1 double one;
1 lark's head knot;
1 double one.
Repeat 8 times to complete the circle.
In each section you have 8 lengths, therefore
16 string threads, numbered from 1 to 16.
With the 8 lengths in the middle, you will make
a flat knot and with the 8 lengths at the
ends, you will make a diagonal double knot
as follows:
Use 7, 8, 9, 10 as core threads or filler
threads. Use 5, 6 and 11, 12 as leader threads
of the diagonal double knot bars.
Use 1 and 16 to form the upper diagonal.
Use 2 and 15 to form the lower diagonal.
Use each length to make the diagonal
double knot bar.

Threads 5 and 6 are the vertical lines in the
middle between 2 bars of cording, on the
left of the central flat knot. They form the
right half of the flat knot in the motif below.
Threads 1 and 2 form the right half of the
core threads of the flat knot of this motif
below.
There are 10 staggered flat knots down the
length. Starting from the top flat knot,
there are 4 complete petal patterns in the
form of a cross, plus a half-cross at the
bottom. When you have made the flat knot
at the bottom which lies level with the
middle of the petals of the last half-cross,
attach all the remaining lengths to the metal
ring with a half hitch. Then either glue them
in position or make an overhand knot at the
end, and cut.
Don't use a very high powered electric light
bulb. Bright lights get very hot and can
cause a fire.

Wall storage hoop

Materials

1 plain wooden hoop
145 m (160 yd) of 4 mm (1/8 in.) diameter jute
1 ball of orange cotton
1 ball of rust cotton
1 ball of mustard cotton

The base

Mount 12 lengths of jute, each 4.60 m (5 yd) long in double reverse lark's head knots on the wooden hoop. Then, on either side of this group, mount successively: 4 lengths 4.20 m (4¾ yd) long (2 on the right, 2 on the left), 4 lengths 4.10 m (4½ yd) long (2 on the right, 2 on the left), 4 lengths of 4 m (4.1/3 yd) long (2 on the right, 2 on the left). From this point, mount all the following lengths to the left of the rest, like this: 2 lengths 3.70 m (4 yd) long, 2 lengths 3.40 m (3¾ yd) long, 2 lengths 3.25 m (3½ yd) long, 2 lengths 3 m (3.1/3 yd) long, 2 lengths 2.90 m (3¼ yd) long, 1 length 2.80 m (3 yd) long.
Threads 23, 24, 25, 26 (counting from the right) form a flat knot, marking the middle of the 1st row of the work. Make 3 flat knots on the right, 3 flat knots on the left of this 1st central knot.
These 7 flat knots make up the 1st row.
2nd row: make 8 alternating flat knots.
3rd row: make 9 alternating flat knots.

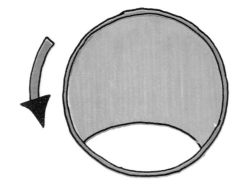

Diagram 1
Work in this direction
on the base

Diagram 2
Make a quarter turn to
the left and work the
storage pockets this way

Continue with alternating flat knots. At the left side of the 18th row of flat knots, attach the 2 threads on the left to the wood of the hoop, in half hitches, attach the 2 threads on the left to the wood of the hoop, in half hitches, slipping the thread which is already attached to the hoop a little further down. Then, at the end of every other row on the left, fasten off 2 threads and let them hang behind the work. You see that each time you come to the end of a row (those on the left only) it is convenient to fasten off the threads as they come up with a half hitch; this allows you to follow around the curved shape, which now returns towards the right as the work moves down. The edge of the rows on the right forms a kind of scallop. This completes the framework of the base. Turn the work half-way around so that the empty section is at the top. Then mount, on either side of the middle of the uncovered wooden circular arc, 6 lengths 2.60 m (3 yd) long (12 lengths in all). Work 3 diagonal double knot bars, bringing the lateral thread from the side towards the middle.

Next, make 3 successive flat knots in the middle. Then pass the 2 knotting threads behind the work and bring them back again, on either side of the flat knot above, so that they form a large pea in relief, held in place by a 4th flat knot beneath the 1st 3.

Start off again with the core threads as leader in a triple section of diagonal double knot bars.

Beneath each of the lower bars of knots, make a knot of knotted chain with the 3 threads nearest the middle (knotted over the 3 lateral threads) which then form a half flat knot.

Finish with overhand knots with 2, 3, 2, 3, 2 threads which you pass through the scallops bordering the base and knot behind.

The pockets

Now make the colored pockets to decorate this base. Call the threads used to make up the base 'natural'.

Pocket 1: Mount on a natural leader:
in the middle: 1 'natural' length 1.10 m (1¼ yd) long;
either side: 5 rust lengths 1.50 m (1¾ yd) long;
either side: 1 'natural' length 1.10 m (1¼ yd) long;
either side: 10 rust lengths of 1.50 m (1¾ yd) long;
at each end, 1 natural length 95 cm (1 yd) long.

Work double diagonal double knot bars with threads 1-2 and 23-24 and with the threads symmetrical to them on the other side of middle, with 5 rust threads over each. Before you do the bar of knots which starts at the middle, make single knotted chains on either side of the middle consisting of 2, 4, 6 then 8 knots; the 1st 2 rust threads near the middle are not included in the knotted chains.

Make a diagonal double knot bar with 10 rust threads on each side. With central threads 12 and 13, which are still inactive, make knotted chains, covering them with their adjacent threads and adding 1 thread on each row. Do this 4 times.

Beneath this motif of knots, make a flat knot with the natural threads. On either side of this flat knot, make 3 alternating flat knots, using, in addition to the 5 threads from the diagonal double knot bar, the 1st thread at the side of the motif of knotted chains (the threads of which pass behind the natural flat knot).

Starting from these flat knots, on either side of the work, work down in diagonal double knot bars which continue until they meet up in the middle, after 1st working the middle of the diamond they are outlining into a double-thread trellis (see the *Glossary*). Make an overhand knot where the 2 natural leader threads meet.

There are still 2 natural threads left beneath the flat knots at the sides. Taking groups of 4 rust threads, work alternately over these 2 core threads knots of a knotted chain, 5 times.

Close up the 2 lateral diamonds with this motif in the middle, with diagonal double knot bars over a natural leader thread. Make a natural flat knot where they meet. With the 10 remaining rust threads on either side of the work, make alternating flat knots to decorate the middle of a half-diamond at the side.

Knot the threads bordering the diagonal double knot bars framing the central 'natural' knot, in 2's into overhand knots. Repeat these overhand knots symmetrically to make the inside perimeter of 2 more diamonds, edged around at the bottom with 2 bars of diagonal double knots. Make a 'natural' overhand knot with the leader threads of these bars of knots at the point where they meet.

Make a 2nd diagonal double knot bar beneath the natural flat knots at the side, over a 'natural' leader thread, formed into a slightly curved shape to join up with the 'natural' overhand knot at the bottom. Then continue

Design:
Marie-Jeanine SOLVIT

106

on in front of it to underline the base of the last central diamond, the middle of which you work into a trellis with 5 threads, 5 times.

Then make a 'natural' overhand knot in the middle of this base. Work the remaining threads on each side into knotted chains, each with 2 and 2 threads, as follows: 7 knots in the middle, 5 at each side, then to finish. Underline this last motif with bars of knots over a 'natural' leader thread, joining up in the middle beneath the spiral braid of the knotted chain with 7 knots.

Pocket 2 (eye-glass case) Mount 12 mustard cotton lengths 1.70 m (2 yd) long over a 'natural' leader.

Taking the 1st thread at each side as leader, do a bar of double knots parallel to the thread bearer with 4 knotting threads from each side. Then cross over the threads remaining in the middle, taking them in groups of 3 threads at the middle and 4 threads after that.

By crossing the threads over in this way, you form a big trellis. Continue that bar of knotting started higher up until it arrives at the point in the middle where the 2 leaders meet. Leave the 4 threads lying to the left and the right of the work to 1 side. Continue the work of the bars of double knots, taking as leaders the threads on the left. Each is knotted in a half hitch over the leader of the diagonal double knot bar right to left from the 1st row, in this way shaping the cross of the bars of knotting. You work 1st with 6 knotting threads, then 5, 4, 3, 2, and the last is knotted at the end over the bar of diagonal double knotting right to left.

Do the same work symmetrically with the threads on the right. Take up the lateral threads (4 from each side). Form 2 Japanese knots with them, then use them to finish off the diagonal double knot on the horizontal. The same leader then returns towards the inside, keeping the horizontal line with the 1st 4 threads.

Using the threads in the middle, make a flat knot with 8 core threads, which, knotted into an overhand knot at the heart of the flat knot, form the central relief.

Repeat symmetrically the work done in the top half of the work. This time, the diagonal double knot bar left to right crosses over the top of the other.

This time, however, the 4 lateral threads do a different motif. The 1st forms a half hitch over the 2nd, the 4th a half hitch over the 3rd. Then the 2 core threads are joined

together in an overhand knot, framed by the same set of half hitches. Repeat this work a 2nd time, after a flat knot which separates the 2 motifs.

Finally, at the middle of the work, make a large flat knot with 2 knotting threads and 6 core threads. Then 2 bars of diagonal double knots join up at the middle with the 5th leader thread. There are still 2 little diamonds to make, with an overhand knot of 4 threads in the middle of each. Finish by an overhand knot with the 4 threads in the middle at the bottom.

Pocket 3 (small round orange one) Mount 12 orange cotton lengths 1 m (1¼ yd) long on a natural leader.

Taking as leaders the threads from either end, make a horizontal double knot bar with 7 knotting threads. Make a large overhand knot with the 8 threads remaining in the middle. Turn this knot so that the threads face you. Lay out 4 to the right, 4 to the left. Knot

them so that they form a bar of knotting which follows the curved shape of the central knot, using as leader threads 6 and 19.

With threads 7, 8 and 17, 18 continue knotting in a semi-circle. Make an overhand knot with the 2 leaders which join up in the middle.

Repeat the work over leaders 5 and 20. Make a flat knot in the middle. Then do a 3rd row of the same work with 4 and 21 as leaders.

Next start work on horizontal double knot bars with threads 1, 2, 3 and 22, 23, 24, working on the 6 threads which spread out like the rays of the sun.

Taking the knotting threads of the central flat knot as leader, then make 2 bars of knots, with 4 knotting threads over each.

Work another horizontal double knot bar with the 2 central threads of the work, after 1st knotting them in an overhand knot.

Pocket 4 (rectangle) You need: 26 m mustard lengths, each 110 cm (48 in.) long and 1 natural string length 2 m (2¼ yd) long mounted in the middle.

Make 2 flat knots at each end and below them a 'Josephine' knot made with 8 threads. Using the 2 threads preceding the 'natural' length in the middle, make 1 knot of a knotted chain over the 2 threads lying on their left. Working towards the left, make 2 knots of a knotted chain with 2 threads, then 3 knots of a knotted chain with 3 threads. Repeat this work symmetrically on the right of the work.

Then, starting from the middle, do a diagonal double knot bar, using the 'natural' thread as leader to underline the motifs above in the work. Make a diamond with a 5-thread trellis in the middle. Do an overhand knot with the 2 leaders where they meet in the middle.

Next, work on each side:* 3 bars of double knotting parallel with that acting as base of the central diamond. With the next 2 threads, make half hitches over the 4 threads above which come from the last bar of diagonal knotting. With the next 4 threads, make 3 flat knots, 1 above the other. Then make a single knotted chain of 3 knots with the 2 following threads, a single knotted chain of 2 knots with the 2 following threads, and 1 more with the 2 following threads. This leaves 5 threads which make the knots of the bar of knotting over the 'natural' leader, which now comes back to the middle of the work, following the base-line of the different knots you have made. * This gives it a slightly curved shape which

climbs up towards the middle at the end. Continue symmetrically, repeating the work from * to * on the right-hand side.

Over the 2 natural threads in the middle, make a large 'pea' (3 flat knots folded over on themselves again to obtain the relief) then * on the left make a diagonal double knot bar over the 'natural' leader which goes at 45° for the work of the 1st 8 threads, then turns horizontally with the 3 following threads.

Before knotting the following threads, make a single knotted chain above of 4 knots, leave 2 threads free, then do a single knotted chain of 4 knots, then 3, then 2. Then continue the bar of knotting upwards until it lies 1 cm (¼ in.) below the preceding 1 on the left-hand side. Return in a zig-zag and make an overhand knot with the natural leader to mark the bottom left-hand corner of the work. Return in a horizontal double knot bar, putting in single knotted chains of 3, then 2, then 1 knot, lined up beneath the chains above the bar of knotting over this row.

With the threads which precede the last thread at this side of the work, make a single knotted chain of 6 knots before the half hitches of the bar of knotting.

Continue symmetrically, repeating the work from * to * on the right of the pocket. Finally, make an overhand knot with the 2 natural threads where they meet in the middle.

Pocket 5. You need: 8 orange lengths 1 m (1 yd) long, 6 orange lengths 1.10 m (1¼ yd) long. Using a 'natural' 20 cm (8 in.) long leader, mount 4 lengths 1 m (1 yd) long, 6 lengths 1.10 m (1¼ yd) long and 4 lengths 1 m (1 yd) long.

Threads 8, 9, 20 and 21 are leaders of diagonal double knot bars, over which you work 5 threads each time. Do another 5 rows of knotting beneath the right to left 1 of leader 8. Work a single knotted chain of 3 knots with the 1st 2 threads on the left of the work. Pass thread 8 around these 2 threads and bring it back to close the diamond with a diagonal double knot bar left to right.

Repeat this section symmetrically in the right-hand part of the work. Make a central flat knot with 2 knotting threads and 8 core threads. Continue with the diagonal double knot bar to close up the diamond. Do a series of overhand knots with 2 threads, starting with the 2 threads in the middle and working up each side to the points where 3 threads remain on the right and left. Make an overhand knot with 2 of them, the 3rd acting as leader for a diagonal double knot bar, which starts off with the 2 threads from the next to last overhand knot. The top 1 of these overhand knots remains on its own.

On either side of the central overhand knot at the bottom, make 2 overhand knots with 2 threads, alternating them so that they are staggered. The descending double knot bar goes around them. The 2 leader threads complete this work by making an overhand knot together.

Finishing

Put these 5 completed pockets onto the base, laying them out as is shown in the photograph. Using a fine crochet hook, pull at the threads through the knots of the base and knot them behind with a flat knot to hold each pocket in place. Still using the crochet hook, weave 1 of the longer threads in and out along the sides to attach to the base in the parts where there is no thread which can be knotted at the back.

The advantage of attaching the pockets on in this way is that it allows you to take the colored pockets off at any time without spoiling anything, either because you want to replace them with something different, or to use them in another piece of macramé. It is advisable to leave a decent length of thread after you have knotted them behind, so that if necessary, you have something to hold onto easily. Slip this length of thread behind the knotting threads of the base with the fine crochet hook, so that you do not see them through the open mesh of the natural base.

The right-hand side of the hoop is still encumbered with surplus lengths of the 'natural' jute (a surplus which it is wiser to leave until this stage). Fasten off each of these threads behind, with a very tight overhand knot, then cut close. However, keep the rest of the threads which are at the bottom in the middle so that you can make 6 arch-shapes with them. These add the final touch to the bottom of your hoop.

To do this, you make — working from the smallest to the biggest — 4 knotted chains in spiral braids with 2 threads, 1 spiral braid of half flat knots (for which you add knotting threads: 2 lengths, each 1.60 m (1¾ yd) long and a final knotted chain in a spiral braid. Starting from the right of the geometric middle, they are attached and finished off on the left.

String curtain

This is a very striking window dressing.
It is 2.20 m (2½ yd) long.

Materials

12 wooden curtain rings
1,870 m (2057 yd) of jute — 110 lengths
each 17 m (19 yd) long
1.70 m (2 yd) of jute for the leader at the
top
14 m (15½ yd) of jute for the 1.70 m (2 yd)
chain acting as a pull cord for the curtain
leader thread 1.70 m (2 yd) long
Divide the 17 m (19 yd) long lengths into
groups of 10 threads each

Method

A

1st group of threads: Mount the threads in
reverse lark's head knots. Form an X with 3
diagonal double knot bars, taking threads 1
and 20 as leaders, then threads 2 and 19, then
3 and 18.
The 3rd bar of knots left to right is crossed
over by the right to left bar to form the
middle of this X motif.

2nd group of threads: Do 2 diagonal double
knot bars, taking as leaders 10 and 11.
Return symmetrically to form the shape of
a diamond. Then 5 cm (2 in.) away and
parallel to the lower sides of the diamond,
make 3 diagonal double knot bars. The top
diagonal bar takes as leader the leader thread
of the bottom diagonal bar from the 3rd row
of diagonal double knot bars of the adjacent
motif on the left — the X motif of the 1st
group.

3rd group of threads: Make a motif similar
to that of the 1st group, in which the leader
of the bottom row of the diagonal double
knot bars right to left continues as leader
of the top row of the diagonal double knot
bars right to left of group 2.
Continue all the way, across the curtain,
repeating these 2 groups.

B

Next, 15 cm (6 in.) lower down, form flat
knots with each group of 4 threads, at
intervals of 3 cm (1¼ in.). Do this 7 times.
Then, 15 cm (6 in.) lower down, repeat the
groups of 3 diagonal double knot bars to
begin the design of the big diamond. Do the
1st point with threads 10 and 11 from group
1. Do the 2nd point, with threads 10 and 11
from the 3rd group. The inserted motif of
the 2nd group is identical to the 1st motif
made with the 1st group of threads in the
work, — the X formed with 3 diagonal
double knot bars, worked in such a way that
you relate them to the adjacent motifs by
the continuity of the leader thread. Put in
a small single diamond, like the 1 done above
in the 2nd group, 8 cm (3 in.) from the
bottom bars of knots of the large diamond,
to make up the central motif.

C

Go back a 2nd time to B, repeat the work
from B to C. Finish, below motif C, with 7
rows of flat knots, like those done higher
up. Let the threads fall free for 22 cm
(8¾ in.) below each of the last flat knots.
Attach large wooden rings on each end and
between each group of 10 lengths (12 rings).
From the rings on the right-hand side of the
curtain, hang a 1.70 m (2 yd) long braid
made from a single knotted chain, to act as
a curtain pull along the rod.

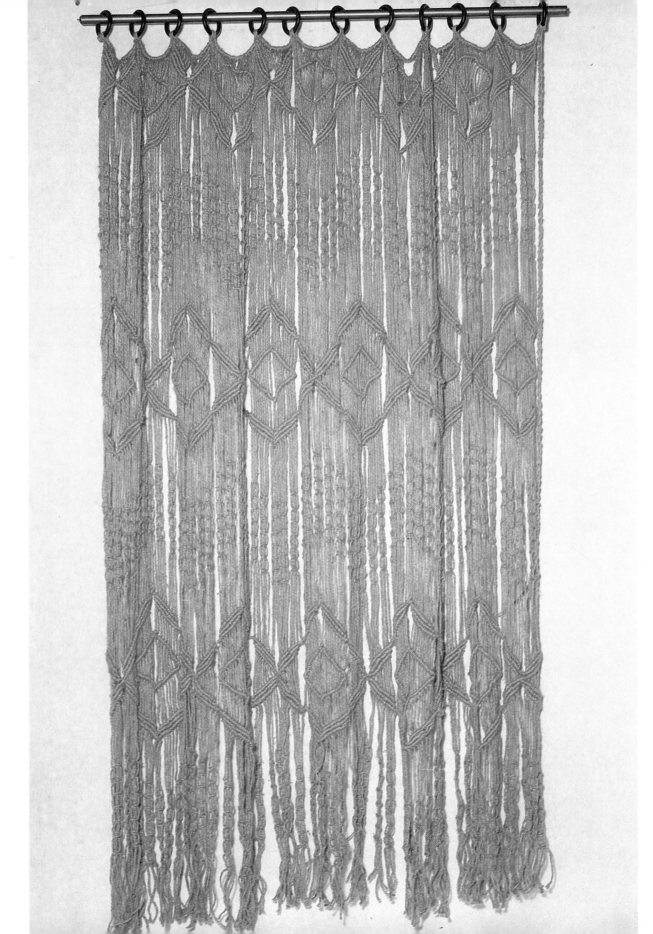

Design:
Maryse DUBOULOIS

Small bag with multicolored beads

This lightweight bag has a braided shoulder-strap made of very fine string.
The beige string gives the bag a rustic look.
This rather whimsical project
has a personality all of its own.

How to bind threads together

Materials

27 lengths of very fine, greyish brown string, each 2.50 m (2¾ yd) long (for the shoulder-strap)
92.10 m (101 yd) of greyish brown string 17 lengths 2.5 mm (1/16 in.) in diameter and 5.40 m (6 yd) long plus 1 length 30 cm (12 in.) long

Method

Front of the bag (see the photograph on on page 115):
Mount 17 lengths on a 30 cm (12 in.) leader thread. You have 34 threads.

1st section: With thread 1 as leader, make a diagonal double knot bar left to right with 5 knotting threads, sloping gently down about 20°. With thread 12 as leader, do the same symmetrically right to left. Repeat this 1st row on the right of the work.

2nd section: With leaders 17 and 18, complete 2 bars of knots sloping parallel to those in the 1st section, with 10 knotting threads over each, finishing where they meet up with the bars of knots from the 1st section. The leaders cross over at this point.

3rd section: Threads 1 and 34 are leaders of diagonal double knot bars, returning towards the middle to form a flattened diamond 14 cm (5½ in.) wide by 5 cm (2 in.)

high. These leaders become core threads of a group of 4 half flat knots, made with the last 2 knotting threads.

4th section: Threads 17 and 18 continue as leaders of diagonal double knot bars and are worked over by threads up to the sides of the work, while 12 and 23 will be leaders of diagonal double knot bars, which start off adjacent to the 1 from the 3rd section, then break away to follow a 45° slope down towards the middle. The knotting threads of the last half flat knot in the 3rd section make half hitches over this diagonal double knot bar.

5th section: Leaders 17 and 18 return from the edges to the middle. All the threads work over them in a undulating diagonal double knot bar, and 17 and 18 cross over each other at their central meeting point.

6th section: Make 4 half flat knots with threads 5, 6, 7, 8 and 27, 28, 29 and 30. Do the same with 11, 12, 13, 14 and 21, 22, 23 and 24.
The knotting threads of these half flat knots form:

1) 2 flat knots with 9 and 10 as core threads on the left and 25 and 26 on the right.
2) The knotting thread next to 4 and that next to 31 become leaders of horizontal double knot bars, over which you knot, on the left, 1, 2, 3 and 4 and on the right 31, 32, 33 and 34.
Frame the middle with 3 half flat knots, each with a single central thread.

7th section: Make 4 half flat knots, with middle threads: 12 and 13 and 22 and 23, taking those around them as knotting threads. On either side of the middle of the work, take 2 of the threads from the flat knots with a single central thread and, bringing the 4 threads together, make 4 central half flat knots.
There is still 1 thread between the 2 groups of lateral flat knots. Use this as the core thread of 3 staggered flat knots.

8th section: Return to the leaders of the horizontal double knot bars in the 6th section and with them make bars of knotting, returning diagonally to the middle and over which 7 threads will work. The 8th and 9th threads then become central threads of 3 half flat knots.

9th section: The last of these 3 half flat knots provides, at the side, the leader of a

Design: Odette SANSONNET

diagonal double knot bar parallel to the 1 in the preceding section and over which you work 7 threads (up to the edge of the work). This same last half flat knot with its knotting threads nearest to the middle, also provides a working thread to make 2 vertical half hitches over threads 12, 13, 14, 15, 16, 17 and 18 and the threads symmetrical to them.

10th section: The diagonal double knot bar from the 9th section returns to the middle, keeping to an angle of about 20°; 9 threads are worked over it in half hitches.

11th section: Take up the 2 threads which cross over each other at the middle of the piece and use them as leaders of 2 rows of knotting, starting horizontally and sloping slightly towards the bottom, with 7 working threads over each (the last 1 being the

leader of the bar of knotting in the 10th section).

12th section: Leave 2 threads free at either side of the middle. The following 1 becomes leader of a wavy bar of knotting up to the outside edge, going down a little at 1st, then climbing up again in a gently curving shape.

13th section: The wavy bar of knotting from the 12th section returns towards the inside on a slope of 20°. Work 12 threads over it. Then take its leader and make vertical half hitches over the 4 threads between it and the middle.

14th section: When you have crossed over the threads which have just joined up at the middle, make more vertical half hitches over the 1st 4 threads (beneath those on the preceding row), then horizontal double knot bars moving away from one another towards the outside of the work.

15th section: The 5th thread away from the middle makes 4 half hitches over the threads on either side of the middle. It crosses over the thread symmetrical to it in the middle, and each starts off in a horizontal double knot bar with 4 knotting threads, while the leader of the bar of knotting in the 14th section returns in a horizontal double knot bar lying alongside the preceding bar. The 1st part of the bag is finished.

You are now at the bottom and are going to continue and make the back of the bag, finishing up with the flap.

You work from the bottom of this bag upwards.

1st section: Complete a horizontal double knot bar right across the work. Make 4 half flat knots at the middle, the 1st 1.5 cm (½ in.) from the horizontal double knot bars.

2nd section: With leaders 1 and 10, then 25 and 34, work cross-over diagonal double knot bars: 1 bar to the edge, the other up to the middle where the leaders cross over one another.

3rd section: Make a horizontal double knot bar from the middle towards the outside.

4th section: Make another bar of knotting, slanting down towards the middle, with only 3 knotting threads, and then return back again to the edge with the same knotting threads.

Take up the middle threads again: make 3 half flat knots framed by 3 other half flat knots. Then leave 3 free threads on either side and finally make 6 half flat knots on either side.

5th section: Make 1 diagonal double knot bar with 3 knotting threads, using as leader the knotting threads of the central knots. Do 1 similar diagonal double knot bar emerging from the following group of half flat knots in the 4th section.

6th section: Make 4 half flat knots in the middle, then a diagonal double knot bar at 20 towards the middle, using as leader the last knotting thread of the 6th half flat knot in the 4th section. Work 5 threads over it symmetrically in half hitches.

7th section: The leader of the lateral bar of knots in the 4th section leads a wavy bar of knots to the inside, over which 11 threads are worked.

8th section: The last knotting threads of the half flat knots in the 6th section are worked in vertical half hitches over 4 threads on each side, forming a curve, the oval shape of which is completed when the same threads make the same vertical half hitches, over the 2 central threads as well.

9th section: The threads lying on either side of this central oval become leaders of diagonal double knot bars, forming a curve which finishes up in the middle with the leaders crossing over.

10th section: Make 2 horizontal double knot bars from the middle to the outside, turn at the ends and return to the middle.

11th section: Make 6 half flat knots with the central threads. Then make vertical half hitches with their knotting threads over the 2 following threads on either side. Then, make 5 half flat knots with threads 10, 11, 12, 13 and their symmetrical threads.

12th section: Use 3 threads from each of the preceding half flat knots as leaders.
1) The nearest to the outside edge on each side leads a bar of knotting running up at 20° to the edge.
2) The nearest to the inside on each side leads a diagonal double knot bar over which you work all the threads up to the middle.
3) The core thread nearest the middle of the work leads a bar of knotting alongside the preceding one.

13th section: The bar of knotting between the 1st part of the 12th section returns to the middle. All the threads are worked horizontally. The leader threads of a 2nd horizontal double knot bar alongside the preceding one cross over in the middle and depart cross-wise with only 4 knotting threads.

You are now at the flap fold-over.

14th section: Now make a series of 6 diagonal double knot bars, using as leaders the 1st and last threads of the work. Tie the 8 central threads 2 by 2 into overhand knots, level with the 2nd bar knotting. With the very fine thread (reserved for the shoulder-strap), bind around 2 cm (¾ in.) of the 1st 2 and the last 2. With the 4 threads in the middle, make 3 half flat knots.
The 1st thread bound around on the left and the last 1 bound around on the right work in half hitches over the leader of the 4th diagonal double knot bar, as well as the knotting threads of the last central half flat knot.

15th section: With the same string you have used for the bag, bind around 2.5 cm (1 in.) of the 8 central threads of the work. About 2 cm (¾ in.) lower down, bind around the threads again, taking in the 4 threads on each side which were the leaders of a last thick diagonal double knot bar lying alongside the 6th of the series in the 14th section. This gives you a central pom-pon of 16 threads. Bind the remaining threads under the last diagonal double knot bar into 3 groups on each side. Thread multi-colored wooden beads in different shapes (round, oval, oblong) onto the very fine string. Attach them to the threads on either side of the group of threads you bound around before the last lot. Hold them in place below with overhand knots under the last bead.
Sew the 2 sides of the bag together using overcast stitch as on the sides and bottom. Make a braid with 27 lengths of very fine string (3 times 9 lengths). Bind around the ends with thread. Attach the bound part level with the top of the flap on each side of the bag, once you have joined the sides together.
Then make 16 pom-pons at the bottom of the bag, bound around at the top with very fine string. Line the bag, but not the see-through open-work of the flap, with a strong fabric in the same color as the string.

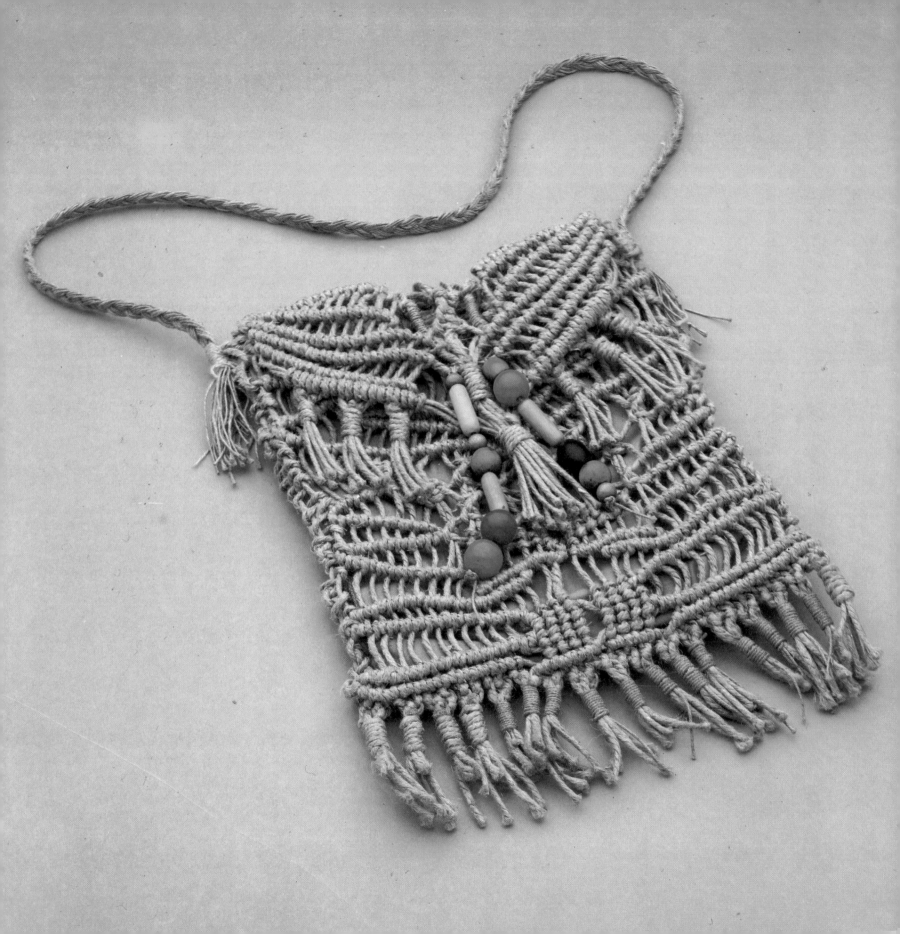

Hanging cradle

*This cradle is a magnificent place for setting
a new-born baby comfortably into its first home.*

A diagonal band of
two staggered flat knots
with double threads.

Materials

Dowelling 3.5 cm (1½ in.) in diameter:
2 lengths 1.30 m (1½ yd) long and 2 75 cm
(¾ yd) long for the top edge
Dowelling 2.5 cm (1 in.) in diameter:
2 lengths 1.14 m (1¼ yd) long and 2 65 cm
(¾ yd) long for the bottom
11.40 m (12½ yd) of webbing for the
bottom — 6 times 1.5 m (1.1/3 yd) and 6
times 1 m (¾ yd)
29.60 m (33½ yd) of sisal string 8 mm
(3/16 in.) in diameter
68 m (75 yd) of macramé cotton, 8 mm
3/16 in.) in diameter
8.80 m (9½ yd) of macramé cotton 5 mm
(1/8 in.) in diameter
985.50 m (1,1084 yd) of macramé cotton
4 mm (1/8 in.) in diameter

Method

The body of the cradle is 0.40 m.
Make notches 1.8 cm (¾ in.) deep by
3.5 cm (1½ in.) wide, 6 cm (2½ in.) from
the ends of the long pieces of dowelling
and 3 cm (1¼ in.) from the ends of the short
ones. Engage 1 piece of dowelling in the
other, the rounded section of the 0.75 m
(¾ yd) length hiding the hollowed-out notch
made in the 1.30 m (1½ yd) length. Hold
the dowelling in place with a thick screw
attached from underneath. Along each long
side, mount 70 lengths 4.50 m (5 yd) long
in reverse lark's head knots. Mount 39
lengths on each short side in the same way.
With a separate 4.50 m (5 yd) leader length,
do a horizontal double knot bar all the way
around, adding 5 lengths 4.30 m (4¾ yd)
long at each corner, likewise mounted in
reverse lark's head knots.

Long side: Starting from the middle, work
2 diagonal double knot bars lying alongside
on each side, followed by a 3rd, 1 cm (¼ in.)
from the 2nd (work towards the outside edge).
Then make a diagonal band of 3 staggered
flat knots, followed by another diagonal
double knot bar, 1 cm (¼ in.) away, then 2
more diagonal double knot bars lying
alongside, and 1 cm (¼ in.) away another
bar of knotting. Then make a diagonal band
of 2 staggered flat knots worked with double
threads.
Then again make 1 diagonal double knot
bar, then 2 bars of knots lying alongside,
after the preceding 1 and before the following
1. These bars of double knots finish at the
side of the work where they meet up in a
point with those symmetrical to them on
the short side.
Next make 1 flat knot, then a braid of 4 flat
knots. Then take the 2nd thread following
as leader of a diagonal double knot bar.
Then use the 6th thread as leader of another
diagonal double knot bar. Next make a
corner of staggered flat knots. Under the
last 2 diagonal double knot bars, make 4
braids of 5 flat knots and a 5th, marking the
corner of the work, where the bars of
knotting from the long and the short side
meet up in a point.
At the middle, make a 3rd diagonal double
knot bar 1 cm (¼ in.) underneath the one's
with which you began the work. Then, make
alternating flat knots, worked in double
threads, to decorate the edge of a diamond,
each side of which is a diagonal band of
these 2 double flat knots, and the middle a
diamond of bars of knotting lying alongside,

Design: Maryse DUBOULOIS

117

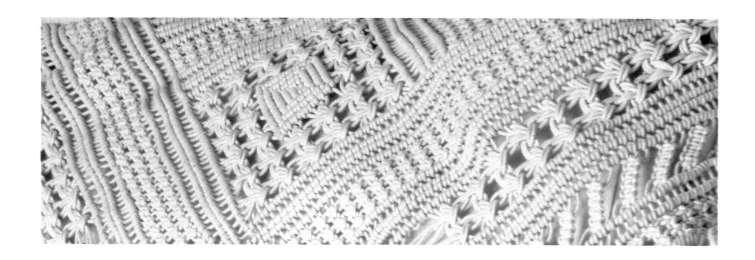

the 1st covered with 8 threads, then the following one's tapering down towards the middle. After the half hitches of the 25th thread on the bar of knots outlining the central diamond, the 26th becomes leader of a bar of knotting which outlines it up to the base where it arrives at the middle of the work.

Then, 1 cm (¼ in.) away, make 2 diagonal double knot bars lying alongside and again 1 bar of knots 1 cm (¼ in.) after those 2. Then make a diagonal band of 3 staggered flat knots, then repeat the pattern of the 4 bars of knotting. Finally, make 3 large alternating flat knots with double threads. Complete this side with half hitches over the 1 m (1¼ yd) length of dowelling. Cut and secure with transparent glue.

Short side: With the 8 central threads, make 2 large flat knots worked in double threads. The 5th thread on either side becomes leader of a diagonal double knot bar, followed by 4 others spaced like those on the long side: 1, 1 cm (¼ in.) space, 2 alongside, 1 cm (¼ in.) space and 1. Then repeat the motif of the braids of flat knots, the 2 diagonal double knot bars and the triangle of alternating flat knots which are symmetrical with the same work done at the end of the long side.

At the middle, after the 4 diagonal double knot bars (still following the same pattern), make a small diamond outlined by diagonal double knot bars, over which you work 11 threads on each side, the 11th thread becoming leader of a bar of knotting outlining the bottom of the diamond. The middle of this motif is worked in alternating flat knots. Underneath its base, the bars of knots move off in the usual pattern. Then 2 rows of large staggered flat knots with double threads follow this motif.

There are 3 large flat knots in a line below the central diamond. On either side, work the 4 diagonal double knot bars again, still following the same pattern, leading them from the outside towards the inside. Finish with 2 triangles of staggered flat knots.

Then tie all the working threads tightly together in half hitches over the 0.65 m (¾ yd) length of dowelling. Secure with transparent glue.

At the bottom of the cradle lay 6 lengths of webbing across 6 widths. Weave them into a trellis and wrap each end twice around the dowelling before securing it with nails.

Now all you have to do is make 4 cords to hang the cradle up by. For each, take 4 1.85 m (2 yd) lengths of thick sisal string 8 mm (3/16 in.) in diameter. With 2.20 m (2½ yd) of 5 mm (1/8 in.) diameter macramé

cotton, make a hook to hang the cradle by (using the technique explained on page 36, with a 10 cm (4 in.) long loop and 4 cm (1½ in.) stem base. Into this base, bind tightly the start of two 8.5 m (3¼ in.) threads, from which you make into a spiral braid of half flat knots, 1.22 m (1.1/3 yd) long with the thick 8 mm (3/16 in.) diameter macramé cotton. Then separate the core threads and wind each knotting thread round 2 core threads. When it is 12 cm. (4¾ in.) long, bring the central threads back into play again and make 7 half flat knots. Then divide them up into 3 groups: one with 2 core threads and 2 with 1 thread. Work a 14 cm (5½ in.) spiral braid of half flat knots in the middle, and 11 cm (4¼ in.) braids for the other two.

The loops for hanging up the cradle must be securely attached to the ceiling. At the other end, slip them over the piece of dowelling which is sticking out by 6 cm (2½ in.)

When each cord is complete, test its strength by pulling on it as hard as you can. If it isn't strong, remake it so that the cradle will be safely suspended.

Slip the loop at the end of the cord over the end of the dowel on the cradle. Nail it in position, so that there is no way the loop can slip off and the cradle fall.

Illuminated head board

Attached above a bed, this head-board
will decorate the wall
and light both sides of the bed as well.

When you uncover the bottom of the lampshade, the light allows you to read; when the light filters softly through the work around the sides and on top, it casts mysterious shadows onto the nearby walls.

Materials

1 2 m (2¼ yd) long wooden rod
2 lampshade frames 20 cm (8 in.) square, placed so that the light-bulb socket is at the top
An assortment of different wools and strings; here is the exact list of those which were used for the head-board pictured:

1 white sports wool: 4 lengths each 3 m (3.1/3 yd)
2 macramé cotton: 2 lengths, each 2.20 m (2½ yd)
3 handwoven mottled sports wool: 1 length 3 m (3¼ yd)
4 unbleached, unwoven wool: 1 length 1.30 m (1½ yd)
5 white sports wool: 1 length 3 m (2.1/3 yd)
6 jute: 1 length 1.30 m (1½ yd)
7 white sports wool: 1 length 3 m (2.1/3 yd)
8 jute: 1 length 3 m (3½ yd)
9 white sports wool: 1 length 2 m (2¼ yd)
10 jute: 1 length 3 m (3.1/3 yd)
11 handwoven mottled sports wool: 2 lengths 1.50 m (1¾ yd)
12 white sports wool: 2 lengths 3 m (3.1/3 yd)
13 handwoven mottled sports wool: 2 lengths 1.50 m (1¾ yd)
14 white sports wool: 1 length 3 m (3.1/3 yd)
15 jute: 1 length 3 m (3.1/3 yd)
16 white sports wool: 1 length 3 m (3.1/3 yd)
17 jute: 1 length 3 m (3.1/3 yd)
18 white sports wool: 1 length 1.60 m (1¾ yd)
19 jute: 1 length 3 m (3.1/3 yd)
20 white sports wool: 1 length 3 m (3.1/3 yd)
21 handwoven mottled sports wool: 2 lengths 3.20 (3½ yd)
22 unbleached, unwoven wool, 1 length 3 m (3.1/3 yd)
23 macramé cotton: 14 lengths 3.20 m (3½ yd) (double mounted)
24 thick sports wool: 2 lengths 2.10 m (2.1/3 yd)
25 thick sports wool: 8 lengths 1.60 m (1¾ yd)
26 thick sports wool: 2 lengths 3 m (3.1/3 yd)
27 macramé cotton: 14 lengths 3.20 m (3½ yd)
28 thick sports wool: 1 length 3.10 m (3¼ yd)
29 thick sports wool: 1 length 1.70 m (2 yd)
30 greyish brown string: 1 length 1.20 m (1.1/3 yd)
31 thick sports wool: 1 length 1.80 m (2 yd)

32 greyish brown string: 1 length 1.10 m (1¼ yd)

33 thick sports wool: 1 length 1.40 m (1½ yd)

34 greyish brown string: 1 length 1.10 m (1¼ yd)

35 thick sports wool: 1 length 1.90 m (2 yd)

36 handwoven mottled sports wool: 2 lengths 3.20 m (3½ yd)

37 unbleached, unwoven wool: 1 length 3.10 m (3¼ yd)

38 thick sports wool: 1 length 3 m (3.1/3 yd)

39 macramé cotton: 2 lengths 3.20 m (3½ yd)

40 thick sports wool: 1 length 3 m (3.1/3 yd)

41 macramé cotton: 2 lengths of 3.20 m (3½ yd)

42 thick sports wool: 1 length 3.10 m (3¼ yd)

43 unbleached, unwoven wool: 1 length 1.20 m (1.1/3 yd)

44 greyish brown string: 1 length 3.20 (3½ yd)

45 thick sports wool: 1 length 8.20 m (9 yd)

46 macramé cotton: 2 lengths 3.20 m (3½ yd)

47 handwoven mottled sports wool: 2 lengths 3.20 m (3½ yd)

48 thick sports wool: 3 lengths 2.90 m (3¼ yd)

49 unbleached, unwoven wool: 1 length 3.10 m (3½ yd)

50 thick sports wool: 1 length 6.90 m (7½ yd)

51 thick sports wool: 1 length 1.50 m (1¾ yd)

52 greyish brown string: 1 length 1.60 m (1¾ yd)

53 thick sports wool: 1 length 1.80 m (2 yd)

54 greyish brown string: 1 length 1.80 m (2 yd)

55 thick sports wool: 1 length 1.80 m (2 yd)

56 thick sports wool: 1 length 1.80 m (2 yd)

57 handwoven mottled sports wool: 4 lengths 3.20 m (3½ yd)

58 thick sports wool: 2 lengths of 3 m (3.1/3 yd)

59 macramé cotton: 14 double lengths 3.20 m (3½ yd)

60 thick sports wool: 1 length 2.10 m (2.1/3 yd)

61 thick sports wool: 7 lengths 1.50 m (1¾ yd)

62 thick sports wool: 1 length 2.80 m (3 yd)

63 macramé cotton: 14 lengths 3.20 m (3½ yd)

64 thick sports wool: 2 lengths of 2.80 m (3 yd)

65 unbleached, unwoven wool: 1 lengths 3.10 m (3½ yd)

66 jute: 1 length 3 m (3.1/3 yd)

67 thick sports wool: 5 lengths 3 m (3.1/3 yd)

68 jute: 1 length 3 m (3.1/3 yd)

69 thick sports wool: 2 lengths 3 m (3.1/3 yd)

70 jute: 1 length 3 m (3.1/3 yd)

71 thick sports wool: 2 lengths 3 m (3.1/3 yd)

72 jute: 2 lengths 3 m (3.1/3 yd)

73 thick sports wool: 1 length 3 m (3.1/3 yd)

74 jute: 1 length 3 m (3.1/3 yd)

75 thick sports wool: 2 lengths 3 m (3.1/3 yd)

76 jute: 1 length 3 m (3.1/3 yd)

77 thick sports wool: 1 length 3 m (3.1/3 yd)

78 jute: 1 length 3 m (3.1/3 yd)

79 thick sports wool: 1 length 3 m (3.1/3 yd)

80 jute: 1 length 3 m (3.1/3 yd)

81 sports wool: 1 length 3 m (3.1/3 yd)

82 thick white sports wool: 3 lengths 1.30 m (1½ yd)

83 very thick white sports wool: 1 length 1.40 m (1½ yd)

84 white sports wool: 3 lengths 1.30 m (1½ yd)

Method

For each side of the lampshade: mount 8 lengths of thick sports wool, 2.70 m (3 yd) long, at the back of the metal strut which holds the light-bulb socket in place, at the middle top.

Mount 10 lengths of the same wool at the front of the same strut. Also mount 2.70 m

(3 yd) plus 2 lengths of 0.80 m (1 yd) very thick, unbleached, unwoven wool.

You need 4 times these quantities, as there are 4 sides of the lampshade to cover in this way.

Mount the 16 lengths on the back alternately on the metal strut: 1 length in a right to left direction, the next in a left to right direction. As for the lengths of unwoven wool, place them as follows: 1 just behind the light-bulb socket, going towards the right, the other just in front, going towards the left. The contrast resulting from mixing the assortment of threads when you lay them out, is further intensified by the fact that, when working with the threads, you avoid repeating any of the knotted motifs.

It would take too long to describe the motifs all one by one. Each of the groups made of fine macramé cotton forms an independant, more classical design, punctuating this unique work with trafitional macramé. The lengths of thick, unbleached, unwoven wool are almost always surrounded by finer threads, which allow parts of the work to be thrown into relief. The lengths of mottled sports wool are often used as core threads, against which the light-colored adjacent threads stand out when used as knotting threads. You can follow the photograph to see the path of the double knot bar which winds along half-way down the work, turns a few centimetres (about an inch) away from the lampshade on the left and returns to outline the cut-away shapes at the bottom. Note the chunky style of the work when the threads used are thick, the finer work when they are thin.

Design: Marie-Jeanine SOLVIT

Join the threads to the metal bar at the top of each lampshade like this.

Group 27 consists of the classical diamond shape, with a filler knot in its middle. Below it, a group of 4 large peas (see the *Glossary*). Underneath, there is a series of knotted chains alternated with free-hanging threads.

After a section composed of some light-colored knots over dark core threads, you come to the section filled with plump rolls of unwoven wool. The curved part at the bottom is made with length 37, which goes up and passes behind the work to join up with 49, and unites this part of the work. The 4 lengths of 57 form large alternating peas, then they go off to right and left in

vertical half hitches over the base of the adjacent light-colored threads. Those on the right lose themselves behind 57, 58, 59 and 60, then reappear.

The lengths of 59 work in double diagonal double knot bars and then combine into a large flat knot. The threads are wound around a ring which you put in horizontally. They are bound together and an overhand knot is tied at the end of each 1.

The lengths of 63 make 2 windmills, separated by a large flat knot.

Length 65 is a belted round diagonal of flat knots decorated with 2 large peas.

The lampshades are securely attached by

means of half-hitches made by the working threads along the top and bottom parts of the frame at the back of the square.

At the bottom of the piece fasten off all the threads with an overhand knot underneath the wavy bar of knotting, but use the longer ones to make decorative pendant trimmings and pom-pons at various points along the base.

Your head-board will be unique because, in addition to the instructions given here, you can add the fruits of your own imagination and inspiration.

Don't use a very high powered electric light bulb. Bright lights get very hot and can cause a fire.

Montgolfier balloon lamp

This makes an original decoration
for a child's bedroom.

Materials

50.40 m (55½ yd) of white macramé cotton,
2 mm (1/16 in.) in diameter
Paper globe lampshade 50 cm (20 in.) in
diameter
1 straw basket 30 cm (12 in.) in diameter
by 20 cm (8 in.) high (these measurements
are those of the basket shown in the
photograph, but if the measurements of
the one you have chosen vary slightly, it is
not important)
Colored wooden beads: 4 large, 8 medium,
64 small
Cotton string, about 2 mm (1/16 in.) in
diameter; about 7 m (7¾ yd) of each of the
following colors: pink, light blue, violet and
dark blue

Method

Prepare 8 lengths, each 6.40 m (7 yd) long,
in each of the 4 colors and 4 lengths, each
2.40 m (2½ yd) long, plus <u>4</u> lengths 8 m (9 yd)
long in white macramé cotton.

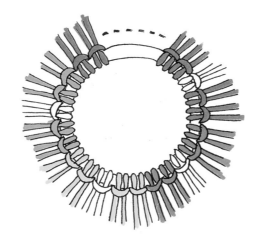

The pattern for mounting
threads on the top ring.

Attach the lengths in lark's head knots onto
a 3 cm (2 in.) diameter ring:
1. 2 lengths in pink, 1 2.40 m (2½ yd) in
   white, 2 in pink
2. 2 in dark blue, 1 8 m (9 yd) in white, 2 in
   dark blue
3. 2 in light blue, 1 2.40 m (2½ yd) in white,
   2 in light blue
4. 2 in violet, 1 8 m (9 yd) in white, 2 in
   violet
5. 2 in pink, 1 2.40 m (2½ yd) in white, 2
   in pink
6. 2 in dark blue, 1 8 m (9 yd) in white, 2 in
   dark blue
7. 2 in light blue, 1 2.40 m (2½ yd) in white,
   2 in light blue
8. 2 in violet, 1 8 m (9 yd) in white, 2 in
   violet
With the white 8 m (9 yd) threads bordered
with pink, make 2 diagonal double knot bars
which move apart, then come together again
to form a pink diamond.
Do the same with the 8 m (9 yd) white
threads bordered with light blue.
Between these motifs, make a flat knot with

the 6.40 m (7 yd) violet threads, bordering 2 white threads, the latter being the core threads.

Then, using the white thread on the left as core thread, make a half hitch over it with the 1st violet thread on its left, then a half hitch over these 2 threads with the 2nd violet on the left, then a half hitch over these 3 threads with the 3rd violet on the left, finally a half hitch over these 4 threads with the 4th violet on the left.

Repeat this motif symmetrically on the right. Then do the whole thing again with the groups of violet and white threads lying opposite on the thread-bearing ring, then with the groups of dark blue threads in between. You have then completed the 1st row all around the central ring.

Continuing on after the pink and blue diamonds with the white thread already laid out in an X, work diagonal double knot bars with: 1st the pink and light blue threads, then the violet and dark blue. The white leader threads then join up with the white threads which formed the middle of the violet and dark blue motifs. Next make a flat knot to mark this meeting point 6 cm (2½ in.) from the central ring. Start off again in a diagonal double knot bar with the knotting threads of this flat knot for leader and forming the diagonal in such a way that the point of the V thus formed lies 15 cm (6 in.) from the central ring.

Make an overhand knot with these 2 white threads. Let them fall free for 4 cm (1½ in.), then make another overhand knot. On either side of this V, there are 4 violet threads, then 4 pink threads, or 4 dark blue threads, then 4 light blue threads. Do another diagonal double knot bar beneath this 1, pulling 1 apart from the other as the threads go down, taking as leader thread, the white thread used as the middle of the flat knot, made 15 cm (6 in.) from the start of the work. This leads to the meeting up of 4 white threads 6 cm (1½ in.) from the 2nd overhand knot.

Then mark the point where they meet with an overhand knot, made with these same 4 white threads.

Work the white threads emerging from the knot in 2 sections. The 1st will be made by forming, with the 2 shortest white threads — those 2.40 m (2½ yd) long — 2 almost horizontal bars of knotting which encircle the globe and over which the groups of 4 threads will be worked with spaces left in between: the 1st group 4 cm (1½ in.) from the central knot, the 2nd 8 cm (3 in.) from this knot. Then these 2 leader threads form

an overhand knot with those of the adjacent motif's leader threads symmetical to them (divided up into 4's around the globe). This overhand knot, directly below the white flat knot made higher up, lies 32 cm (12¾ in.) below the top ring. Thread a medium-sized violet thread (here 2 cm (¾ in.) in diameter) onto the 2 white threads. Keep it in place with an overhand knot underneath, followed by a spiral braid of a single knotted chain with 16 knots. Then thread the 2 threads through a large bead (here, 4 cm (1½ in.) in diameter) held in place by an overhand knot using the 2 threads.

Perpendicularly above this beaded motif, start off on the 2nd diagonal double knot bar underneath the flat knot lying 6 cm (2½ in.) away from the central ring, by attaching on each side a 2.10 m (2.1/3 yd) length, either in violet or dark blue depending on the color of the threads already there (mount in lark's head knots). You now have 4 new threads. Join them up in an overhand knot 10.5 cm (about 4 in.) from the central ring. Then, while the core threads hang free, the 2 knotting threads divide up and pass behind the 1st of the 4 threads which are stretched between the bars of knotting you have already made. They come back back and form around their core threads a spiral braid of half knots left to right, 9 cm (3½ in.) long, after which the threads of this braid split up into 2's to go join up, on either side of the medium-sized violet bead, with the white threads which met in the bead (see the photograph).

Now, on either side of the overhand knot at the point of the V made 15 cm (6 in.) from the central ring, 2 2.10 m (2.1/3 yd) lengths come and add their light blue color to the middle of pink threads (or pink to the middle of light blue threads). Attach these with 2 half hitches to each of the white leader threads that they meet (see the photograph, upper right motif). These new threads come between the pink or light blue threads which were worked 4 cm (1½ in.) from the central knot.

Here you start the 4 colored suspension ropes which support the car of the balloon (2nd section of the work). The 2 threads which are still unused from the big overhand knot with 4 threads spread apart in diagonal double knot bars.

Take, as an example, the motif in which you have 1st, on each side, 2 pink threads, then 4 light blue, then 6 dark (either violet on the left or dark blue on the right). With the pink threads, make 2 half hitches over the white leader, then a single knotted chain of

15 knots. With the light blue threads, make 4 half hitches, then 12 half flat knots. With the dark threads make a braid 2.5 cm (1 in.) long, then 1 1 cm (¼ in.) long. The white leader thread returns towards the middle and all the colored threads attach themselves to it in half hitches. Now make an overhand knot at the middle with the white threads, which again separate to be worked over in half hitches by the colored threads.

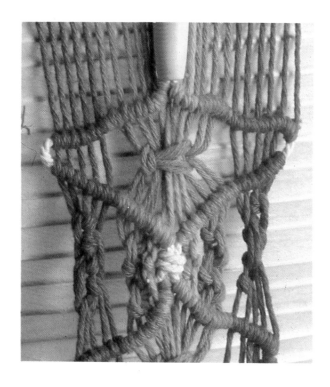

Make a flat knot with the 4 light blue threads and with the next 4 dark ones, then 2 alternating flat knots (a pink and light blue and a dark and light blue), then a pink flat knot in the middle, a light blue on each side, a pink and light blue and finally a central pink 1.

Follow the base line of this point of flat knots with a bar of knotting to return to the middle, where a long natural colored vertical wooden bead (here, 5 cm (2 in.) long) joins up the 2 leader threads.

When these emerge, they break away from each other into gently sloping diagonal double knot bars (about 20°), then come together again to form a wide and flat diamond with a flat knot, with 4 pink, 4 blue in the middle and 2 knotting blues on either side, in the middle.

This diamond is closed at the bottom by an overhand knot with the white threads. This knot is framed by a single knotted chain of 3 knots in pink, a double knotted chain of 4 knots in light blue and a dark double knotted chain of 5 knots, formed alternately over the central thread.

Then comes another wide and flat diamond like the 1 made higher up, but this time its white leader thread follows the wavier shape of a horizontal union.

At the base of the triangle, the leader thread starts off from the middle again to form a bar of double knots, curved around in a dome shape.

There are now 4 pink threads which are almost used up. Thread them through a medium-sized violet bead, which is held in place with an overhand knot beneath it. Do a half hitch over the 1st light blue thread with the adjacent thread. Then make a half hitch with the 3rd over the 1st 2, then a half hitch with the 4th over the 3 1st ones, and a half hitch over the 4 light blue threads with the 1st violet. This frames the violet bead with a motif reminiscent of 2 half-open curtains.

The white leader threads return in a diagonal double knot bar to the middle and form an overhand knot there.

On either side, the dark thread is nearly exhausted. So, thread it through a small

124

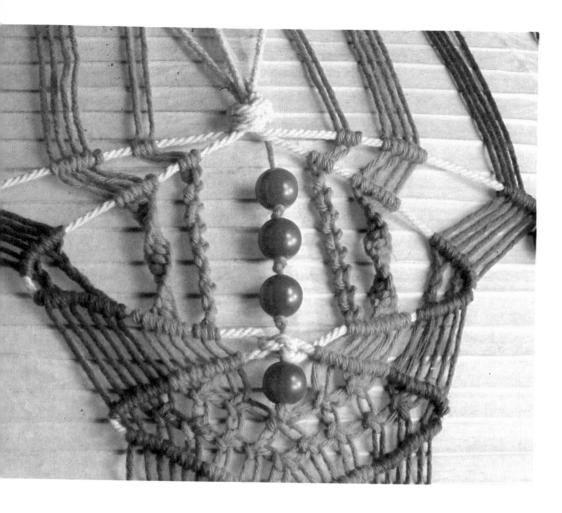

threads as leaders.

With the white central threads, do 1 overhand knot with 2 threads, 1 overhand knot with each thread, 1 overhand knot with 2 threads, 1 overhand knot with each thread and an overhand knot with 2 threads.

To frame this white middle, make on each side: a single knotted chain of 12 knots (light blue), a single knotted chain of 14 knots (light blue and dark), a single knotted chain of 16 knots (violet), a single knotted chain of 18 knots (light blue and dark). The base line of these chains dictates the slope of the diagonal double knot bar which follows and is doubled up by a 2nd bar of double knots. The leader is the 1st central light blue thread.

Return towards the middle, after making a central flat knot of 2-8-2 threads with the white leader, then the light blue leader (1st light blue thread at the side). Make 2 overhand knots, 1 above the other, with the white threads to close the diamond, then at either side, single knotted chains like the 1's above the diamond, with 6, 8, 10, 12 knots.

Bind all the threads together, keeping them all in the right position to emphasize the rounded shape, with the white middle threads, which form the body of a pom-pon with 6 rows of white threads in double thickness. Knot behind and keep a length of white thread to attach to the car.

Finish with 4 12 cm (4¾ in.) spiral braids of half flat knots, taking the dark threads as core threads so that you get 4 light blue spiral braids.

Repeat these sections I and II all round the white globe. There will be 4 of each.

Next, attach a string of pink and dark blue beads, separated by overhand knots, either side of the medium-sized violet bead up above. Attach the ends of the thread to the white V with 2 half hitches.

Then attach 4 pink beads separated by overhand knots onto a vertical pink thread, and attach it behind the overhand knot made with 4 white threads (see the photograph). Attach the 4 pom-pons an equal distance apart around the edge of the basket-car, by passing the lengths of white thread you have saved for this purpose through the cane. Bring the threads back through the cane to the front so that you can make loops to hang around the ship. For each scallop, make a white cable with a single knotted chain of 32 knots. Keep the excess threads on the inside of the basket to make it easier to replace the paper globe or basket later.

pink bead, and hold it in place with an overhand knot. Then thread on a small dark blue bead which you secure with a double overhand knot.

Cut off what remains of this dark thread. On either side of the central white knot, make single knotted chains: or 3 light blue knots, 5 light blue, 7 dark, 9 dark. The white leader threads move away from each other in diagonal double knot bars at 45°. Then each thread, starting with the light blue nearest the middle, is used as leader of a new double knot bar, after which the white threads return in a diagonal double knot bar towards the middle to frame this filled-in motif. At this point, make a white overhand knot in the middle, followed by a single knotted chain of 6 knots.

Make 5 flat knots with the dark threads, 8 flat knots with the light blue threads and

cross these 2 braids over, the light blue passing in front of the dark 1. Hold them in place at the bottom with a bar of double knots, the leader thread of which starts off from the side and is the first dark thread on the outside of the last dark flat knot. Continue with 3 more rows of double knots, immediately beneath the 1st, which lead back all the dark threads towards the middle of the motif. Make the last half hitches over each double knot bar with the white threads. These threads become leader threads for 2 bars of diagonal double knot bars, returning towards the middle.

A tall diamond is thus formed, the middle of which is worked into a trellis (see the *Glossary*) with double dark threads.

Do another 3 bars of double knots, working from top to bottom, beneath the last 1 worked like this, and using 3 light blue

Folding screen with four panels

*This unique screen is ideal for privacy or
to set off a striking piece of furniture.*

Materials

Instructions are given for 1 panel. For the
complete screen, you have to allow 4 times
the quantities given if you want to make a
screen with 4 panels like the one shown in
the photograph. Each panel is 37 cm (15 in.)
wide and 145 cm (58 in.) high.
So, prepare:
5 times the height of the screen, in double
lengths, 10 x 145 cm (58 in.) = 14.50 m
(16 yd) per screen. You need 32 of these
lengths.
This makes: 14.50 x 32 = 464 m (510½ yd)
of white macramé cotton for each panel plus
1 wooden screen frame (here painted black).

Method

The 2 lengths at either end are mounted in
reverse lark's head knots (that is, with the
loop behind, not in front). When mounting
these 2 lengths, they should be folded so that
one end is about 25 cm (10 in.) longer than
the frame. The 2 short ends are the filler

or core threads, and do no work at all. The
longer threads go on the outside.
The half flat knot (1st half of the formation
of a flat knot) gives you a spiral braid worked
around the filler threads.
Mount the 28 lengths included in the 2
independant spiral braids on the sides in
double reverse lark's head knots.
At *either* end of the work, work 15 cm
(6 in.) of half flat knots (spiral braid), then
15 cm (6 in.) of flat knots, then 12 half
flat knots, 13 cm (5¼ in.) of flat knots,
13 cm (5¼ in.) of half flat knots, 11 cm
(4¼ in.) of flat knots, 12 cm (4¾ in.) of
half flat knots, 12 cm (4¾ in.) of flat knots,
13 cm (5¼ in.) of half flat knots, 13 cm
(5¼ in.) of flat knots, 11 cm (4¼ in.) of half
flat knots, 11 cm (4¼ in.) of flat knots.
This brings you down to the bar along the
bottom of the frame. Finish off with a half hitch.
Do 14 flat knots, then stagger the 2nd row
(see the photograph). In the middle of the
8th row of staggered flat knots, work 2
diagonal double knot bars, which end
up, 27 cm (31 in.) lower down at the end of

Design: Maryse DUBOULOIS

A simplified plan of
the central motif.

the panel. Work vertical columns of flat knots in groups of 4 threads (7 flat knots in each column). At either end, continue the columns: the ones at the ends are made up of 9 flat knots. Those made with threads 9, 10, 11, 12 and 53, 54, 55, 56 have 17 flat knots.
The diagonal double knot bars starting from the middle of the work meet up with the 9th flat knot of the column above (where threads 13 and 52 are knotted).
Let threads 14, 15, 16, and so on, up to 51 hang free.
With the central threads, work a diagonal double knot bar 5 cm (2 in.) lower down, parallel to the preceding 1, to form the frame around the central flat knot. Threads 14, 15, 16, 17, 18, 19 and 46, 47, 48, 49,

50, 51 remain free, and are only used for the lower outside framework of the central motif. This central motif is a flat knot made with 6 core threads (or filler threads) and 2 groups of 7 threads for the knot itself. Repeat symmetrically the double framework with diagonal double knot bars, 5 cm (2 in.) away from each other. Again work the columns of 7 flat knots as in the top section of the frame.
Then make 2 diagonal double knot bars with the lengths from either side of the work which return to cross over in the middle. Continue with the staggered flat knots, as in the beginning, using what threads there are until you reach the 1st complete horizontal row. From this point, continue with the staggered flat knots for 47 cm (19 in.).

Next, work 7 diagonal double knot bars in a chevron pattern, then 14 vertical columns, each of 7 flat knots, then 7 bars of diagonal double knot bars. Let 5 cm (2 in.) of thread hang free at this point. Then make 7 diagonal double knot bars, 2 rows of flat knots, 7 diagonal double knot bars, 5 cm (2 in.) of free threads, 7 diagonal double knot bars, 14 vertical columns, each of 7 flat knots, 7 bars of diagonal double knot bars. Finish with staggered flat knots down to the lower part of the frame, over which you fasten off each thread with a half hitch. Sew in the ends at the bottom, and then glue the threads to make sure they are finished off securely.
Repeat the same work for each of the 3 remaining panels.

128

Indoor tree

Many people like to decorate a room with a tree in a pot.
But should it always be a live tree?
Why not use a pear tree like this one,
made with an old umbrella frame
and terracotta and ceramic pears?

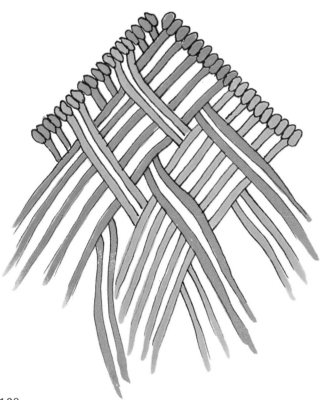

An example of the
trellis pattern worked
with unevenly divided-
up threads

Materials

A large old umbrella
1.20 m (1.1/3 yd) length of bamboo at
least 3 cm (1¼ in.) in diameter.
A straw basket 33 cm (13¼ in.) in diameter
and 30 cm (12 in.) high, filled with gravel
or pebbles from the seashore.
A ceramic bird (with a hole in the bottom
so that you can put it on a metal spike of
the umbrella)
A ceramic tortoise to go at the foot of the
tree
A small ring, 3 cm (1¼ in.) in diameter, to
start off the work
16 ceramic pears 6 cm (2¼ in.) high
8 rings, 7 cm (3 in.) in diameter
528 m (581 yd) of natural-colored macramé
cotton
455 m (500½ yd) of natural-colored rug
wool

Method

Strip the fabric off the umbrella frame. Hold
the end of the umbrella ribs in a vertical
position by means of threads knotted onto
the shaft, from which you have previously
removed the curved handle.
Mount 16 lengths, each 6 m (6¾ yd) long,
on the ring which has been slipped over the
metal point at the top. Do a 1st row all
around of flat knots, then beneath each,
another which has as core threads the 2
threads of the preceding knot plus the metal
stem of a rib. On the following row, make
alternating flat knots, then again a flat knot
on the stem of a rib.
At this point, add 8 lengths, each 6 m (6¾ yd)
long, making an overhand knot about 1.5 cm
(½ in.) from the point where it is folded in
2, then make a 2nd overhand knot 1.5 cm
(½ in.) lower down. The loop formed by
doing this is passed up behind the flat knot
lying between the ribs. Bring the 2 ends of
the length through the loop lying between
the 2 overhand knots and, keeping the loop
and the 1st overhand knot vertical, make a
flat knot, the 2 core threads of which will be
those of the added length.
Now, 2 threads remain besides each metal rib.
Wrap each 1 around these ribs with 2 half
hitches.
On the following row, each of the 2 inserted
lengths becomes leader of a short descending
diagonal double knot bar, covered by half
hitches from the 2 adjacent threads.
These diagonal double knot bars join up in
a flat knot which takes in the rib as the 3rd
core thread. The 2 threads remaining between
these flat knots make a single knotted chain

of 4 knots. Then they will be used as core threads of a flat knot which adopts the last knot of the single knotted chain as a button in its middle.

And, again make a flat knot on each rib. On either side of the button, add a 5.80 m (6.1/3 yd) length of rug wool, using the same technique to insert it as with the preceding lengths, so that 16 vertical loops appear on the work, resembling 16 young leaves on a tree.

You now have groups of 10 threads between the ribs.

Make the 1st part of a windmill with these 10 threads, stopping the pattern after the diagonal double knot bar left to right which starts from the middle of the windmill. Pass the 2 threads 1 and 2, 9 and 10 from each group around the ribs beside them and form a flat knot with 2 knotting threads on each side and 6 core threads.

These same threads make, alternately, a knot of a bar of knotting over the rib in the following way: each of the ribs, lying as they are between 2 flat knots, will be covered again by the double knotting of a thread from the knot lying on its left. Leave 4 threads in the middle of each group. Use these as the middle of another big flat knot with 3 knotting threads on each side.

Next, split up the 4 core threads into 2's and take them towards the ribs at the sides. There, they join up with the core threads of the adjacent motif, forming a flat knot clasping the rib in its middle.

Continuing to follow the same technique of inserting lengths, putting another 'leaf' into the air on either side of the central flat knot — that is, add 16 lengths, each 5.80 m (6.1/3 yd) long. Make 3 flat knots on the following row, then staggered flat knots. At the edges, therefore only 3 threads are left. Knot these as a flat knot with a single core thread. The following row is a horizontal double knot bar, the leader of which is a thread laid out around this metal frame and which forms a half hitch over each rib.

Next, make 2 rows of staggered Japanese knots (see instructions for this knot on page 12). Onto the double thread which ties the bottom of 1 row to the top of the following row, add a 6 m (6¾ yd) length of macramé cotton. This makes: 8 lengths in each motif between ribs 64 lengths in all. With these new threads, make 3 flat knots, then 3 rows of staggered flat knots all around the circumference.

Each motif between ribs now includes 2 groups of staggered flat knots, laid out on either side of the middle of the motif, as follows: 3, 2, 1. This gives 2 points directed towards the bottom. These are underlined with diagonal double knot bars which follow their contours (see the photograph). The leader thread of these bars of knots is a thread of rug wool knotted over a rib and then attached to each of the following threads by a half hitch. At each point (top or bottom) of this chevron, add a 6 m (6¾ yd) length of rug wool — 36 lengths. Make a 4 cm (1½ in.) braid at the middle of each motif and at the level of the ribs; then use a length of wool as the leader of a horizontal double knot bar. This leader is

This loop and knot leave a good relief shape

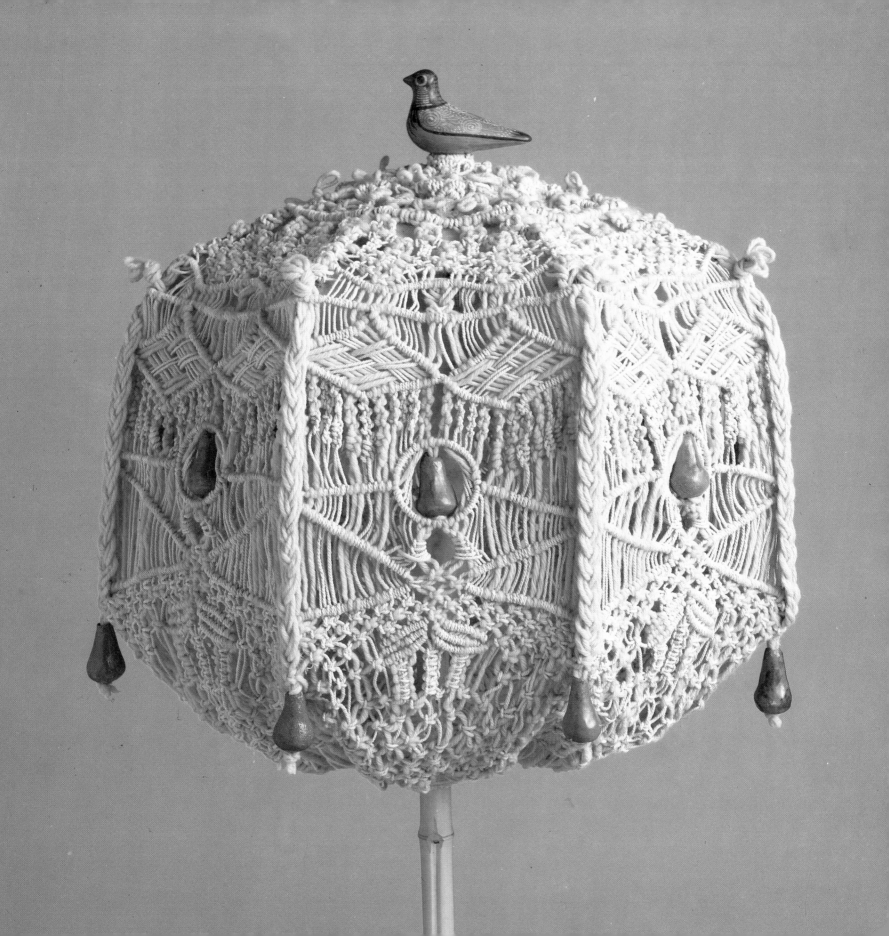

wound around each rib; it is 2.08 m (2.1/3 yd)
long. Under each of the lower points of the
bar of knotting in a chevron pattern on the
row above, add a 3 m (3.1/3 yd) length of
cotton (16 lengths). This will be the leader
of diagonal double knot bars, forming
diamonds with an overhand knot in each
corner.

Work the middle of the diamonds into a trellis
(see the *Glossary*) alternating 4 threads with
2. Below, make braids of single-knotted
chains before inserting 8 rings, 1 at the
middle of each motif. Over each ring, make
half hitches with 8 threads. Use the 2 core
threads to attach a pear at the middle.

The 8th thread becomes leader of a horizontal
double knot bar which turns behind the rib
and returns towards the middle in a diagonal
double knot bar.

The 1st knotting thread over the ring comes
down to be knotted just after the 8th, and
the others likewise, to look like an open
curtain around the pear. Beneath the ring,
make 5 vertical half hitches, each incorporating the threads of the 1 before, a flat knot
in the middle, followed by 2 alternating
knots. From here, make gently sloping
diagonal double knot bars lead away,
followed by 3 rows of alternating flat knots.
You now make triple diagonal double knot
bars with the core threads as leaders and
7 knotting threads over each.

Beneath these bars of knots, make a braid
of flat knots with the 6 core threads and
1 on either side with 5 threads. Make 6 knots
in the braid in the middle, 5 in the braids
at the sides. Around them, make alternating
flat knots which are more spaced out.

Continue with these until you are 12 cm
(4¾ in.) below the central braid. Finish
with consecutive flat knots, each incorporating
all the threads of the preceding row, until
the threads are exhausted.

Put the handle into the bamboo and to
keep it in place, bind all the threads around
the bamboo. You then use some transparent
glue. Cut off the surplus threads.

Level with the top of the diamonds, mount
onto each rib (same technique of vertical
loops), 3 1.80 m (2 yd) lengths of wool
and make a braid, threading it through
when it falls level with the last diagonal
double knot bar, bringing it back again
underneath the next flat knot so that you
can hang a pear on it. Finish with an
overhand knot. Cut.

Stick the bamboo into the pebbles in the
basket and put the bird on the top of the
tree, slipping the umbrella point into the
hole at the bottom of the bird; then put
the tortoise at the foot of the tree.

Design: Marie-Jeanine SOLVIT

134

Glossary

Binding or tying around. Holding several threads tightly together by means of a binding thread which is wound around them several times to the required length.

Braid. A column of consecutive knots which can be made up of flat knots, half flat knots (it then falls in a spiral), alternating half hitches, knotted chain, and so on.

Butterfly. Coiling up the threads in the form of a figure 8 to shorten the lengths while you are working.

Button. Overhand knot made with the core threads of a flat knot after the 1st half flat knot and before the second. This fills out the middle of a flat knot with a round ball.

Cavandoli work. Macramé worked in 2 colors: 1 for the base, the other for the motif. The knots are those used for bars of knotting. The threads of the base work in horizontal half hitches (double knots), and the threads of the motif in vertical half hitches. The motifs are laid out, like those for cross stitch in embroidery, in little squares, but when the work is done, the design you get in macramé is more elongated than the one drawn out on the squares of the pattern. This type of knotting, which is closely worked, looks as though you have taken a lot of time and trouble to do it and resembles embroidery.

Core threads. Threads kept taut and still while the threads framing them are knotted around them. Also called *central threads* or *filler threads.*

Decorative knot. Knots which may be quite complex, featuring a rhythmic design motif which is complete in itself. Examples of decorative knots are: Josephine knot and Japanese.

Double row of knotting. Two rows of knotting, one on top of the other.

Flat knot (also square knot). A right-hand half flat knot, followed by a left-hand half flat knot, working over a non-active thread. The basic flat knot is made with 4 threads: 1 knotting thread on the left, 2 non-active core threads and 1 knotting thread on the right. But it can include 1 or several core

135

threads and 1 or several knotting threads.

Gathering (collecting) knot. One of a group of threads knotted around the others to hold them together forms this knot.

Half hitch (Double knot). 2 consecutive loops made side by side by the knotting thread over the leader (you use this knot to make bars of knotting).

Half flat knot. The 1st of the 2 halves which together make up a flat knot. The "right-hand half flat knot" is one in which the knotting thread on the right passes in front of the core threads. The "left-hand half flat knot" is one in which the knotting thread on the left passes in front of the core threads.

Holding cord. Thread, usually horizontal, over which the lengths are attached at the beginning of the project. Depending on what you are making, the "holding cord", which is also called a "leader thread", can be a metal thread, a stick, a cane or any other material chosen to support the macramé.

Knot of a bar of knotting. See half hitch.

Knot of a knotted chain. Knot broken up into 2 parts: thread on the right does a single knot over the thread on the left and *vice-versa*. A single knotted chain consists of 2 threads. A double knotted chain is formed by knots made with 4 threads, worked in pairs.

Knotting thread. The one which forms the knots.

Lark's head. For mounting a length on its bearer: the loop marking the middle of the length is placed in front of the bearer, then the 2 threads which are hanging down are passed behind the bearer and brought back to the front through the loop.

Leader thread. Thread which is held taut so that the other threads can work over it, especially in all types of bars of knotting (also called *knot bearer*).

Length: A piece of thread of a fixed length. The length is folded in 2 before being mounted on its thread bearer. Each length in a macramé project is therefore twice as long as each of the 2 pendant threads making it up.

Overhand knot. The thread is brought around into a loop and the end is passed through this loop. An overhand knot can be made with 1 or several threads; they are then worked together as 1.

Pea or large pea. A pea forms a loop in relief. It is a braid of flat knots (generally 6) the core threads of which are passed behind the work and brought back to the front above the 1st knot of the braid. It is kept in its rounded position in relief by a 7th flat knot made underneath. Also known as a *bead*.

Starting point. (Picot edging). Different beginnings for decorative knots, adopted to form a loop above the holding cord. These knots are made with the threads of each length folded in 2, before attaching the length onto the holding cord.

Pyramid. A succession of flat knots getting larger and larger, each one incorporating all the threads which made up the 1 before. Eventually, the motif widens out into a 'pyramid' shape.

Reverse Lark's head knot. For mounting a length on its bearer as defined in the last paragraph, but this time placing the loop behind the bearer and passing the threads in front of the bearer, then taking them to back through the loop. The lark's head loop is also known as the "reversed double half hitch".

Row of knotting. Double knots (half hitches) tied closely together on a leader thread looking somewhat like 2 beads threaded onto a taut thread. Also known as *ribbed bar.*

Row of diagonal knotting. Double knots (half hitches) tied closely together over a taut leader thread lying obliquely. The top part of the oblique thread is always mentioned first; so a "diagonal double knot bar left to right" describes an oblique leader thread starting from the top left-hand side and running down to the bottom right. Conversely, a "diagonal double knot bar right to left" describes an oblique leader thread starting from the top right-hand side and running down to the bottom left. Also known as *diagonal double knot bar.*

Row of horizontal knotting. Double knots (half hitches) tied closely together over a taut leader thread lying horizontally. Also known as *horizontal double knot bar.*

Row of vertical knotting. Double knots (half hitches) tied closely together over a taut leader thread lying vertically.

Section. Group of knots forming a part of the work. Dividing up the instructions in this way in a lengthy piece of work allows you to establish consecutive stages which do not necessarily correspond with horizontal "sections" working from top to bottom of the work, but which break it up into distinct parts which are easily marked out.

Simple knot. One thread forms the 1st part of a half hitch — that is, a single loop over a non-active adjacent thread. This is the knot, which, when alternated, makes a knotted chain.

Single row of knotting. One row of knotting.

Splice. The addition of a thread to lengthen one that is too short or has broken in the course of the work. In a bar of knotting, the 2 threads are laid head to tail and covered over together with half hitch knots. At the middle of a flat knot, the length to be added is joined to the core threads and bound up tightly with them when the flat knot is knotted.

Thread. Word used to describe a single length of macramé material, whether cotton, wool or any other kind of fibre.

Thread bearer. See *Holding cord.*

Trellis. A criss-cross of threads as in weaving or darning. This is usually done with threads lying in the middle of bars of knotting arranged in a diamond, square or circular shape.

Triple row of knotting. Three rows of knotting, one on top of the other.

Windmill. X-shaped cross of diagonal double knot bars, preceded and followed by shorter bars of knotting.

Index